PR

What the Bible Is All About for Women

Lisa truly loves the Word of God, and it shows as she illuminates the truth in a way in which we can all relate. This devotional is anything but boring and is a must-read for any woman desiring to know more about the Bible!

KIM HILL
Worship Leader and Recording Artist

Lisa Harper is passionate about Scripture and equally passionate about ministering to women. She combines both loves in *What the Bible Is All About for Women*, infusing a classic devotional book with fresh insights for women of today.

MAX LUCADO
Best-selling Author and Minister

Lisa Harper is brilliant! Our conversations are always intellectually stimulating, culturally relevant and just a whole lot of fun—which is exactly what you get in this book. Lisa writes as if you are sitting on the back porch laughing, reading and studying together. And for the right price, I'll give you her cell phone number so she can come and join you!

CHONDA PIERCE
Christian Comedian
Recording Artist and Author, INO Records

If anyone can help us to hear, understand and receive the truth of Scripture, it is Lisa Harper. Her God-given ability to not merely teach the Word but package it in a way that stirs the heart and calls to action is incomparable. When she speaks, ears perk up. When she puts pen to paper, the soul stands at attention to listen.

PRISCILLA SHIRER
Speaker and Author, *He Speaks to Me* and *Discerning the Voice of God*

In a day in which people deeply connect with stories and yet too often find the Bible abstract and irrelevant, Lisa shows us that the 66 books of the Bible are telling one grand story of personal and cosmic redemption, with Jesus starring as the lead character. She invites us to find our stories in God's unfolding big story as the gospel of His unfathomable grace heals and liberates our broken and foolish hearts.

SCOTTY SMITH
Author and Founding Pastor, Christ Community Church
Franklin, Tennessee

I am hungry most all the time. I have looked to food, relationships, entertainment, shopping, ministry, my children—you name it, I've tried to satiate my starving soul with it. When will I get it that God allows me to experience aching emptiness so that He can satisfy my deepest cravings? *What the Bible Is All About for Women* is a loaf of bread and daily manna for the female soul that was created to be filled by "every word that comes from the mouth of the Lord."

LISA WHELCHEL
Best-selling Author, *Creative Correction, The Facts of Life and Other Lessons My Father Taught Me* and *Taking Care of the "Me" in Mommy*

What the BIBLE is all about for Women

A Devotional Reading for Every Book of the Bible

LISA HARPER

Regal

From Gospel Light
Ventura, California, U.S.A.

Published by Regal Books
From Gospel Light
Ventura, California, U.S.A.

Library of Congress Cataloging-in-Publication Data
Harper, Lisa, 1963-
What the Bible is all about for women : a book of devotions / Lisa Harper.
p. cm.
ISBN 978-0-8307-4406-0 (kevlar)
1. Bible–Devotional use. 2. Bible–Introductions. 3. Christian women–Religious life.
I. Title.
BS617.8.H37 2007
242'.643–dc22
2007000914

1 2 3 4 5 6 7 8 9 10 / 10 09 08 07

Rights for publishing this book in other languages are contracted by Gospel Light Worldwide, the international nonprofit ministry of Gospel Light. Gospel Light Worldwide also provides publishing and technical assistance to international publishers dedicated to producing Sunday School and Vacation Bible School curricula and books in the languages of the world. For additional information, visit www.gospellightworldwide.org; write to Gospel Light Worldwide, P.O. Box 3875, Ventura, CA 93006; or send an e-mail to info@gospellightworldwide.org.

Contents

Acknowledgments

I'm very grateful for Cheryl Green, my literary agent, and Naomi Duncan, my booking agent. Both have been an endless source of encouragement and advocacy. Without their hard work, I'm quite sure the only people listening to my stories would be relatives! I'm also grateful to the professors at Covenant Theological Seminary. They illuminated the truths and promises in God's Word in such a way that I "see Him bigger" as a result of their tutelage.

INTRODUCTION

Welcome to the Greatest Love Story Ever Told

I often meet people whose experience with Bible studies has been about as interesting as watching paint dry. One friend told that me she stopped attending the study at her church because she had a hard time not giggling at the sea of bobbing heads around her—the result of so many people falling asleep! Others have told me how they were made to feel like spiritual pygmies when they asked a question about something they didn't understand in the lesson. While some of those worst-case scenarios are humorous, it's not at all funny when people who are seeking a more intimate relationship with God end up thinking the Bible is boring, inexplicable or irrelevant.

God's Word is anything but boring—it is a stirring literary masterpiece! It's packed with dramatic plots, fascinating narrative and beautiful poetry. It's also full of joy, comfort and tangible hope. It can be mysterious and difficult to decipher, but *it is certainly not dull*!

In the early 1950s, renowned Bible teacher (and wearer of enormous flowered hats) Henrietta Mears had a big idea: to write an overview of the entire Bible that would help everyday Christians understand how the story of Scripture fits together and points to Jesus. That big idea became the book *What the Bible Is All About*, which has been through about a gazillion editions to date and continues as one of the most popular guidebooks for Jesus followers adventuring through God's Word.

You hold in your hands a devotional based on that remarkable book, just for women. And while you should know that I'm not and will never be the great Henrietta Mears, I have tried here (to the best of my ability) to continue her legacy of talking about Scripture in words that anyone can understand, with a generous helping of humor on the side. Henrietta believed that God meant His Word to be a gift for *everybody*—not just people with thousand-dollar vocabularies—and that any teaching about it should be accessible and practical. I wholeheartedly agree.

Whether you're a seasoned woman of faith, a brand-new believer or just beginning to explore who God is, this devotional was written to help you deeply engage with God's Word. Each chapter focuses on one book of the Bible, and while this may seem a bit intimidating at first, I think you'll be surprised at how satisfying it is to walk through God's Word one step at a time. I recommend tackling one book of the Bible (that is, one chapter from this book) per week, although there are a few very short books that won't take you that long!

After a brief story to introduce each book, here's what you'll find as we journey together through Scripture:

1. **What's the *Story* of This Particular Book?** This section is a bird's-eye view of the action. We'll take a look at some high (and low) points and explore the broad theme(s) of each book.

2. **Henrietta's Highlights.** This section consists of Henrietta's synopsis and suggested Bible readings, and contains some memorable quotes from Dr. Mears.

    - *Synopsis*: In chapter 1 of *What the Bible Is All About*, Henrietta wrote, "each book has a message, and we should endeavor to discover what that message is." Here you'll get her in-a-nutshell summary of what each book tells us about Jesus.

    - *Suggested Bible Readings:* This section breaks up each book into daily readings so that you can easily cover one book of the Bible per week. For books that are quite short, readings are broken up over only one or two days.

    - *Memorable Quotes from Dr. Mears.* Here, I've included a few excerpts directly from the original *What the Bible Is All About*, just so you know I'm not making this stuff up!

3. **Looking for Yourself in God's Love Story.** These are a few questions to consider as you study each book. Take some quality time to think and pray about what the Holy Spirit wants to teach you through God's Word, and write your reflections in a journal or diary. Think of this as the "travelogue" of our journey into Scripture or a collection of snapshots that you can revisit again and again.

4. **Movie Clip Moment.** I believe it is our responsibility to move toward unbelievers and engage our world to reflect God's compassion for the lost. This is one of the reasons I've suggested a movie clip at the end of each chapter. It's a simple way of taking something familiar in culture and pointing back to our Creator. Plus, I think it helps us recognize just how compelling, relevant and colorful God's Word really is—that it's not just some boring old textbook! Please know that I have tried to include qualifications when necessary (such as warning if the suggested clip is inappropriate for children) to shield you and your family from undue awkwardness. But ultimately, I encourage you to use your own wisdom and sensibility with this interesting (but sometimes inflammatory) juxtaposition of film and faith.

Henrietta wrote that as we begin to study the Bible, we will find that "a unity of thought indicates that one Mind inspired the writing of the whole series of books; that it bears on its face the stamp of its Author; that it is in every sense the WORD OF GOD." In other words, as we dig into the Book that is the written revelation of God, we will get to know Him—*that* is what the Bible is all about! My prayer is that you will get a clearer picture of Jesus Christ and how very much He loves you—and that you'll find *yourself* in the miraculous, redemptive storyline that runs throughout Scripture!

Warm regards,

Lisa

Who Has the Lion's Share of Your Heart?

The Old Testament story of Abraham and Isaac offers an incredible life application lesson on worship. Abraham was a man of faith—in fact, four verses in chapter 11 of Hebrews are spent recounting his character. He walked away from his friends and homeland because God said so. He earnestly followed God's divine MapQuest directions, even though he'd never traveled so far before. For the most part, Abraham obeyed God and adored his family. But he was by no means a *perfect* man.

You may remember that Abraham's son, Isaac, was born to fulfill a promise that God made to old Abe and his wife, Sarah. He was the child they thought they'd never have, not in their wildest dreams. They actually laughed at the prospect. They just couldn't imagine buying Pampers when they were both wearing Depends! But the Bible says that Isaac was born when Abraham was 100 years old.

Can you imagine their complete amazement and delight when Isaac bellowed his first cry? They probably fought over who got to change his diapers, and I'll bet they never took him to Mother's Day Out. Isaac's name literally means "laughter" in Hebrew and he was certainly the joy of their lives. Thus, Abraham's heart sank when God asked him to sacrifice his beautiful, long-awaited son.

> Then God said, "Take your son, your only son, Isaac, whom you love, and go to the region of Moriah. Sacrifice him there as a burnt offering on one of the mountains I will tell you about" (Genesis 22:2).

I'm sure the depth of Abraham's sorrow was as great as the joy he had experienced pacing outside the delivery tent. Yet he was obedient—Scripture tells us he got up early the next morning and saddled his donkey. Although I've wondered if part of the reason he left at the crack of dawn was to avoid Sarah—because how in the world was he going to come back home with her only child's blood on his cloak and explain what he'd done?—Abraham certainly had a long journey to make. He had plenty of time to worry about his wife's reaction as he trudged through the desert, because the region of Moriah was three days away. I can't begin to imagine how incredibly hard that hike was.

> When they reached the place God had told him about, Abraham built an altar there and arranged wood on it. He bound his son Isaac and laid him on the altar, on top of the wood. Then he reached out his hand and took the knife to slay his son (Genesis 22:9-10).

You probably know the rest of the story. God provided the greatest gift Abraham could have imagined in the form of a ram wrapped in a thicket. That auspicious animal was the perfect substitute for a burnt offering. Old Abraham probably cried during the barbecue because he was so thankful he didn't have to slay his own son. This true story had a very happy ending.

But why do you think God asked Abraham to go through that terrible journey and contemplate such a gut-wrenching sacrifice in the first place? I think this poignant imagery illustrates how we're supposed to love God *above all else*. I think Jehovah was reminding Abraham that while he was called to be the best daddy he could be to his darling boy, Isaac still wasn't supposed to be his *first* love. Worship was never intended to be horizontal, it was always meant to be vertical. God is supposed to get the biggest chunk of our heart and mind.

What's the *Story* of This Particular Book?

"Genesis" comes from a Greek word meaning "beginning" or "generation," which is appropriate as this is both the beginning of God's redemption story and the beginning of the Israelites' (the people group God chose to be His very own) *generational history*. As a matter of fact, this book covers more time (from Creation to 1804 B.C.) than all the other books of the Bible combined! Genesis is also the first volume of the "Pentateuch," which includes the first five books of the Old Testament that God revealed through Moses (the first five books of the Bible are also sometimes referred to as "The Law").

In his first outing as an author, Moses recounts the beginning of time and space (see Genesis 1); the initial rebellion of humanity against our Creator (see Genesis 3); the history of Adam and Eve's descendants (see Genesis 4–11); God's blessing of Abraham and the establishment of Abraham's legacy (see Genesis 11–25); the formation of Israel's 12 tribes (see Genesis 29:31–30:24; 35:16-20); and about a million other amazing things!

Henrietta's Highlights on Genesis

Her Synopsis

Genesis Portrays Jesus Christ, Our Creator God

Her Suggested Bible Readings

Sunday: *Creation* (Genesis 1:1-5,26-31; 2:7-22)
Monday: *The Fall* (Genesis 3)
Tuesday: *The Flood* (Genesis 6:1-7; 7:7-24; 8:6-11,18-22; 9:1-16)
Wednesday: *Beginning of Languages* (Genesis 11:1-9)
Thursday: *The Abrahamic Call and Covenant* (Genesis 12; 13:14-18; 15; 17:4-8; 22:15-20; 26:1-5; 28:10-15)
Friday: *Story of Joseph* (Genesis 37; 42)
Saturday: *Jacob's Final Blessing* (Genesis 49)

Memorable Quotes from Dr. Mears

"Genesis is the record of human failure, first in an ideal environment (Eden), then under the rule of conscience (from the Fall to the deluge) and finally under patriarchal rule (Noah to Joseph). In every case of human failure, however, God met human need with marvelous promises of sovereign grace."

"God called all things into being by the word of His power. He spoke and worlds were framed (Hebrews 11:3)."

"A very large portion of the story of Genesis is devoted to Joseph (Genesis 37–48). Why? Because Joseph is the link between the family and the nation. Up till the time of Joseph it is a family, the family of Abraham, Isaac and Jacob. . . . The moment we turn over the page and step into Exodus it is a nation, not a family."

"The book of Genesis ends in failure. The last words are in a coffin in Egypt. Death only marks the pathway of sin; the wages of sin is death (Romans 6:23). The people needed a Savior!"

Looking for Yourself in God's Love Story

1. Read Genesis 1:1-25. List your top three favorite things God made in this passage, and then explain why you chose them.

2. Read Genesis 1:26-27. Spend some time thinking about what's so significant about God being an "Us" and write down your thoughts.

3. Read Genesis 15. When is the last time you felt like Abraham—*Okay, God, I've read all these incredible promises in the Bible, but I don't see any of them coming true in my life. How can I be sure that You really will provide for me?*

4. Read Genesis 49:29-33. Why do you think Jacob wanted to be buried in Canaan instead of Egypt? Where do you want to be buried and why?

Movie Clip Moment

The Lion, the Witch and the Wardrobe is a popular movie based on the first book in a series called *The Chronicles of Narnia,* which was written by C. S. Lewis, one of the twentieth century's best-loved storytellers. These "children's books" by Mr. Lewis have inspired millions of kids *and* adults with their vivid depictions of divine themes! This allegorical film follows the lives of four precocious English children who find an armoire in an attic, which leads to a magical land called Narnia. While Narnia is, of course, a fictional place, its breathtaking beauty, imaginative characters and the sweeping theme of good versus evil parallel some of the colorful true tales in the first 50 chapters of God's story!

Biting the Hand That Feeds You

My stepdad, John, isn't what you'd call a true gambler—I don't think he's ever even been to Vegas or Atlantic City—yet he faithfully buys a lottery ticket once a week. And sometimes he'll talk about how all his problems will vanish just as soon as he wins the "big one." I don't think he's alone in assuming that his life would be enhanced by winning some elusive lottery. Based on the billions of dollars Americans spend on scratch-and-win tickets, roulette games and Powerball, it's evident that lots of folks think a winning lottery ticket would fund a magical escape from their troubles and transform their lives into a dream-like existence. But they're wrong.

A New Jersey woman named Evelyn won the New Jersey lottery *two* times (1985 and 1986) for a total windfall of $5.4 million. However, today she's dead broke and lives in a trailer. Another woman, named Suzanne, won large ($4.2 million) in the Virginia lottery in 1993, but she later borrowed against her assets and lost even bigger. She's also dead broke now. Ken Proxmire won a cool million in the Michigan lottery. Five short years later, he filed for bankruptcy. Another Michigan lottery victor—named Willie—won $3.1 million in 1989. After a two-year spending spree (allegedly cocaine was his favorite purchase), he'd not only lost his cash, he'd also lost his freedom as a result of being formally charged with murder.

And those are just a few of the stories about real-life lottery winners who tumbled into despair not long after posing for a picture, holding a giant cardboard check and wearing an ear-to-ear grin. Simply Google "lottery winners" and you'll find a long list of people who experienced divorce, bankruptcy and disillusionment soon after cashing their first dividend check. It seems "good fortune" actually causes most people to make really foolish choices.

That same theme certainly resonates throughout biblical history. Instead of prompting gratitude and praise, "good times" typically bred spiritual *carelessness*, a *callousness* toward others and *casualness* in their mission among God's people. Getting what they wanted was usually followed by a regrettable season of self-centeredness and self-destruction.

What's the *Story* of This Particular Book?

Exodus reads like an Indiana Jones adventure movie, with Moses playing the lead role (see Exodus 2–3)! The overarching storyline is that of God's *provision* and *protection* for His people. He provides a miraculous escape from Egypt (see Exodus 7–13); He protects them against Pharaoh's pursuing army (see Exodus 14); He provides food for them to eat and water to quench their thirst (see Exodus 16); He provides a tailor-made campsite at Mount Sinai (see Exodus 15–18); He protects their hearts for Him and the health of their community with guidelines for righteous living (see Exodus 19–31); and the list goes on. But rather than responding to this divine windfall of blessing by bowing to their Creator in humble gratitude, the Israelites make a stupid fake cow and bow to it instead! Their deplorable behavior makes Moses so mad that he hurls the first set of commandments to the ground, shattering them, and then has to haul his tired self all the way back up the mountain to inscribe a second set (see Exodus 32–33).

Henrietta's Highlights on Exodus

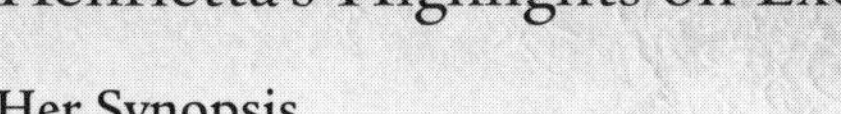

Her Synopsis
Exodus Portrays Jesus Christ, Our Passover Lamb

Her Suggested Bible Readings
Sunday: *Bondage* (Exodus 1)
Monday: *The Call of Moses* (Exodus 3–4)
Tuesday: *The Plagues* (Exodus 7:20–10:29; 11)
Wednesday: *The Passover* (Exodus 12)
Thursday: *The Law* (Exodus 20)
Friday: *The Worship* (Exodus 25:1-9; 28:1-14,30-43)
Saturday: *Moses' Commission Renewed* (Exodus 33:12–34:32)

Memorable Quote from Dr. Mears
"Exodus is preeminently the book of redemption in the Old Testament. It begins in the darkness and gloom, yet ends in glory; it

commences by telling how God came down in grace to deliver an enslaved people, and ends by declaring how God came down in glory to dwell in the midst of a redeemed people."

Looking for Yourself in God's Love Story

1. D. L. Moody once observed that Moses spent 40 years thinking he was somebody, 40 years learning he was nobody, and 40 years discovering what God can do with a nobody. How has God impressed these same lessons on your heart?

2. Read Exodus 13:17-22. God isn't one of the guys who whispers sweet nothings in the dark and then pretends not to know us when others are around. Instead, God advertises His affection for us—He went so far as to use a floating bonfire to publicize His special relationship with the Israelites! In what specific ways has God revealed His love for you recently?

Movie Clip Moment

The Ten Commandments, directed by the legendary Cecil B. DeMille in 1956, is a must-see movie! Mind you, the special effects are laughable, the costumes are gaudy, there are more than a few discrepancies between the Old Testament text and the script (plus you'll forever have a mental picture of Charlton Heston as Moses if you watch it) but it's still worth it because this is one of the greatest adventure stories in history brought to life in the grand scale of old Hollywood. It makes the book of Exodus pop right off the page—you'll never again read Israel's escape from Egypt with resigned boredom! And *The Ten Commandments* is a family-friendly movie that mom and dad can watch with the kids.

Sacred Isn't Spelled S-T-I-F-F

My friend Teresa Sugar bounced into my office one morning and erupted into giggles as she set her guitar down. (For years she led worship and I taught at a weekly Bible study.) She'd just gotten back from a trip to a small Southern town and couldn't wait to tell me a comical story she'd been told during her stay.

Teresa told me that while visiting a church where she was a guest vocalist, she met a woman named Mary who'd brought her entire family to attend the church social several years before. When Mary's youngest son, Jimmy, had announced that he wanted to sing a solo during the program, Mary was thrilled, assuming her five-year-old wanted to sing the B-I-B-L-E song they'd been practicing at home.

Mary beamed when Jimmy's turn came and he bounded on stage with enthusiasm. But when he grabbed the microphone and began to sing, her parental pride turned to mortification, because instead of sharing a wholesome VBS ditty, Jimmy began to belt out the lyrics of the Hank Williams Jr. song "A Country Boy Can Survive."

If you haven't listened to that country classic in a while, one of the more memorable lines is: "We make our own whiskey and our own smoke, too, ain't too many things these 'ole boys can't do!"[1]

I chuckled along with Teresa as I pictured that poor mama's expression when her mischievous kindergartener started crooning about cigarettes and whiskey, thereby shattering the somber mood in the Southern Baptist church! Children seem especially gifted when it comes to embarrassing their parents in spiritual settings, where most adults act stuffier than usual. And I couldn't help thinking that actually isn't such a bad thing—because sacred and stiff aren't supposed to be synonymous anyway!

What's the *Story* of This Particular Book?

The book of Leviticus (also called the book of Laws and most likely recorded by Moses while the Israelites were hanging out at the base of Mount Sinai) is filled with rules about how the Jewish priests were supposed to facilitate worship, as well as a very long list of responsibilities for God's people. And because of all the particulars, Leviticus isn't what you'd call a real page-turner! But if you think about it, these holy regulations aren't really boring; they're *redemptive*—they illustrate how impossible it is for us to remember, much less follow, every single minute detail of the Law; therefore, they point to our need for a Savior to rescue us from the penalty of breaking it! Attempting to live perfect lives according to the very letter of the Law leads to self-righteous rigidity. Acknowledging our innate imperfections and trusting in the sufficiency of Christ's substitutionary death on the cross lead to glorious freedom!

Henrietta's Highlights on Leviticus

Her Synopsis

Leviticus Portrays Jesus Christ, Our Sacrifice for Sin

Her Suggested Bible Readings

Sunday: *Burnt Offering* (Leviticus 1)
Monday: *The Priests* (Leviticus 8)
Tuesday: *Pure Food Laws* (Leviticus 11)
Wednesday: *The Day of Atonement* (Leviticus 16)
Thursday: *The Feasts of Jehovah* (Leviticus 23)
Friday: *God's Pledge* (Leviticus 26)
Saturday: *Dedication* (Leviticus 27)

Memorable Quotes from Dr. Mears

"The book of Leviticus is God's picture book for the children of Israel to help them in their religious training. Every picture pointed forward to the work of Christ."

"What we bring is our sin; what Christ brings is the offering and atonement for sin."

Looking for Yourself in God's Love Story

Read Leviticus 25. If we celebrated a relational Year of Jubilee, what "debt" would you be most thankful for being released from?

Movie Clip Moment

Jack Nicholson plays Melvin Udall, an obnoxious, obsessive-compulsive writer in the 1997 romantic comedy *As Good As It Gets.* And while I don't recommend it as a family film because of adult themes, there are lots of funny—yet sad—scenes depicting the madness and isolation that come with trying to follow too many rules. (Keep in mind as you're watching that God's laws in Leviticus are intended for His people's good, and don't in themselves lead to mental illness!)

An Expedition to Remember

My sister and I went through a big scare not long ago when our father (Everett Harper) was diagnosed with colon cancer and scheduled for emergency surgery. We both flew to Orlando as quickly as we could to be at his side. Fortunately the surgery went well and within a few days his doctors gave us good news about his prognosis. But there were a few moments between that first alarming phone call and the physician's postoperative report when the situation seemed pretty grim—when Dad was convinced that his time on Earth was drawing to a close.

In one of those sober moments, I was alone with Dad in his hospital room when he started talking about his prospective funeral. He told me that he didn't want to be buried in Florida—where he's lived his entire adult life—but would prefer to be buried in Alabama or Tennessee (he grew up in Knoxville, Tennessee, and has always loved hunting in Alabama where my sister and her family live). I listened patiently and then replied, "Dad, we'll take you wherever you want to go, but if you choose Alabama or Tennessee, you'll probably have to be cremated."

He grunted—Dad's not real talkative, we often tease that I got his extra words—and then sort of snorted, "I don't want to be cremated." I sighed and responded, "Well, Dad, if you insist on having an out-of-state service, I think that's the only option." The room was silent for a minute while he considered my comment; then he looked at me ever so seriously and said, "I want you to take my truck [he's a contractor, so his truck is not unlike the Lone Ranger's trusty steed] and put me in the back. Then drive my body up to Alabama. They have permits for that kind of thing."

I grinned and shook my head—thinking the morphine was making him a lot more "colorful" than usual—and told my old-fashioned father that toting his body down the Interstate in a Chevy wasn't an option for me. That I'd be in therapy for the rest of my life if I took a trip like that! I can only imagine the mortified stares I'd get from other drivers while speeding down the highway with my dad in tow—not to mention the more serious attention of state troopers along the way—though it would certainly be an expedition to remember!

What's the *Story* of This Particular Book?

Numbers is the story of the incredibly colorful, four-decade-long expedition the Israelites took after escaping from Egypt's clutches. Their desert ramblings include so many wondrous eye-popping events and so many woeful eye-rolling events that even the 36 chapters of this book are really just the abridged version—a condensed collection of agony and ecstasy trip memories! God prepared His people for this epic journey at Mount Sinai (see Numbers 1–9); then they walked—essentially in circles—for 39 long years in the Wilderness of Paran (see Numbers 10–21); and finally made it to the entrance of the Promised Land (Numbers 22–36). This 40-year odyssey saw the death of one generation and the birth of another. In the process, God ordered Moses to take two censuses (see Numbers 1:46; 26:51) in order to keep track of everybody—hence the name of the book, Numbers. (As was customary in that culture, only men who were old enough to qualify for military service were actually counted.)

Henrietta's Highlights on Numbers

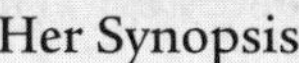

Her Synopsis
Numbers Portrays Jesus Christ, Our "Lifted-Up One"

Her Suggested Bible Readings
Sunday: *The Guiding Cloud* (Numbers 9:15-23)
Monday: *The Report of the Spies* (Numbers 13:16-33)
Tuesday: *Israel's Unbelief* (Numbers 14)
Wednesday: *Water from the Rock* (Numbers 20:1-13)
Thursday: *The Brazen Serpent* (Numbers 21:1-9)
Friday: *Balaam's Feast* (Numbers 22)
Saturday: *The Cities of Refuge* (Numbers 35:6-34)

Memorable Quotes from Dr. Mears
"Numbers is also called the Book of the March and the Roll Call. It might, too, be called the Book of Murmurings because from

beginning to end it is filled with the spirit of rebellion against God."

"Here were about 3 million people on a sterile desert, very little grass, very little water, no visible means of support. How were they to be fed? God was there! How were they to trace their way through a howling wilderness where there was no path? God was there! God's presence provides everything!"

Looking for Yourself in God's Love Story

1. Read Numbers 21. In what way does the unique "prayer pole" in this Stephen King-ish story remind you of the Cross? (For a hint, read John 3:14-15.)

2. Read about the real Mr. Ed (remember the television show about the talking horse?) in Numbers 22. How would you diagnose Balaam's spiritual shortcomings?

3. Read 2 Peter 2:15-16. When you can't see around the corner of your circumstances, do you tend to charge forward–like Balaam–or are you more inclined to pull the covers over your head and hope problems will magically disappear? Describe a circumstance in which God told you to *walk* and one in which God told you to *wait*.

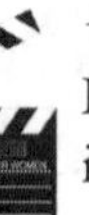

Movie Clip Moment

I can't believe I'm actually recommending this movie–but it is arguably the best film ever made about a trip in which everything that could go wrong does! The 1983 comedy *Vacation* chronicles the madcap journey of the Griswold family, who've set out on a cross-country quest to visit the theme park Walley World–the dad's (Clark Griswold, played by rubber-faced comedian Chevy Chase) idea of the Promised Land. The misadventures portrayed in this movie come close to rivaling the ups and downs of the Israelites' sojourn from Egypt to Canaan–although this fictional American family doesn't whine or grumble nearly as much as God's dysfunctional people!

Straight-Shooting Son of a Gun

Last year I was invited to be on the cover of *Today's Christian Woman.* I was tickled and humbled by the honor, and thrilled that the magazine had hired a great make-up artist and photographer in Nashville for the cover shoot. On my big day I was plucked and fluffed and powdered. Then I was framed and posed and strategically lit. In the end I was shaded and airbrushed. And when I saw the final cover mock-up, I was delighted by the digital enhancement, because my wrinkles and waistline were much less noticeable. They didn't *drastically* alter my appearance—it was just a cuter, more condensed version of me!

A few days after the issue hit the stands, I went over to my best friend Kim's house. When I walked in, she was standing at the sink and her nine-year-old, Benjamin, was sitting at the kitchen table doing his homework. And right there, prominently displayed next to his math papers, was the magazine. Kim grinned at me and then said, "Hey, Benji, look who's on the cover of that magazine!"

He glanced at it and asked innocently, "Who is it?"

Realizing that her brag-on-Lisa plan wasn't working out very well, she said with a chuckle, "Benji, you *know* who that is!"

To which he replied, "No, I don't, Mom."

Obviously embarrassed, Kim responded with just a hint of rebuke, "Benjamin, that's Lisa on the cover."

He looked back down at the magazine for a long moment, then looked up and retorted dryly, "Well, she never looks like that when she comes to our house."

Much like Benjamin, Moses was a man who didn't mince words—he always told the truth, even when it stung! And the book of Deuteronomy records three of his most straightforward speeches to the children of Israel. Moses' honest discourse served to encourage the weary sojourners, galvanizing them for the final push into the Promised Land and preparing them for the transition to Joshua's leadership. It also served as the old guy's good-bye.

What's the *Story* of This Particular Book?

Deuteronomy is the last book of the Pentateuch, and its title literally means "copy of the law," or "second law." If this collection of final addresses by Moses had titles, they'd probably be something like: "God's Faithfulness Throughout This Wild and Wearisome Journey" (see Deuteronomy 1–4:43); "Don't Forget to Read His Directions" (see Deuteronomy 4:44–26); and finally, "Here Comes Joshua!" (see Deuteronomy 27–31). When he finished clearly communicating everything he had to say to his giant Jewish team, this wonderful old coach tilted his weathered face toward the heavens and began to sing. And only after blessing each Israelite tribe and praising God did dear Moses finally go gently into the night (see Deuteronomy 32–34).

Henrietta's Highlights on Deuteronomy

Her Synopsis
Deuteronomy Portrays Jesus Christ, Our True Prophet

Her Suggested Bible Readings

Sunday: *Forward March* (Deuteronomy 1:6-46)
Monday: *Instructions* (Deuteronomy 5; 6:4-18)
Tuesday: *The Messiah, Prophet* (Deuteronomy 18:15-22)
Wednesday: *God's Covenant* (Deuteronomy 30)
Thursday: *The Song of Moses* (Deuteronomy 32:1-44)
Friday: *God's Blessings* (Deuteronomy 33)
Saturday: *The Death of Moses* (Deuteronomy 34)

Memorable Quotes from Dr. Mears
"These noble orations were given as he stood on the great divide between his earthly and heavenly life. He was looking from the top of Mount Pisgah over a century crammed full of epoch-creating events. Then he turned his gaze upon the future of the people he was about to leave."

"The Christian heart always quickens its beat when it comes to Deuteronomy, for this book was a favorite with our Savior."

Looking for Yourself in God's Love Story

1. God's people were absolutely exhausted by this point in their providential journey from Egypt to the Promised Land—they were in desperate need of the encouraging words Moses spoke. When's the last time "someone in charge" communicated much-needed encouragement to you?

2. Read Proverbs 18:21. When have you spoken *words of life* into someone else's weary heart?

Movie Clip Moment

Mr. Smith Goes to Washington (1939) is a very popular old flick—it's been deemed "culturally significant" by the Library of Congress and selected for preservation in the United States National Film Registry—that stars a young Jimmy Stewart. (Many say this motion picture is the vehicle that made him a major star.) Interestingly, the movie is directed by Frank Capra, the same man who directed Mr. Stewart in *It's a Wonderful Life*. The main context of *Mr. Smith Goes to Washington* is American politics and the main theme is "Good Guys Really Can Make a Difference." There's a great scene midway through the movie that takes place on the Senate floor, where Jimmy Stewart (playing Senator Jefferson Smith) makes an impassioned speech that's reminiscent of Moses, the divinely inspired orator of Deuteronomy!

Guided by Gratitude

One of my favorite authors is a white-haired sage named Brennan Manning, who really seems to "get" God's grace. I pick up whatever he writes the minute it hits the shelves! He's an anointed storyteller, and I think one of the best stories he tells is the one about how he got his name. He talks about how he developed a close friendship with a young man named Ray Brennan when they were both soldiers in the Korean War. He describes one snowy night in January 1952, when he and Ray were huddled inside a bunker just a few hundred yards from enemy lines. This is what Mr. Manning said happened next:

> We were passing a chocolate bar back and forth. Ray took the last bite when a grenade lobbed by an undetected North Korean landed squarely in the center of the bunker. Ray was the first one to spot it. Almost nonchalantly he flipped the candy wrapper aside and fell on the grenade. It detonated instantly. His stomach smothered the explosion. I was completely unharmed, untouched. He looked up at me, winked, and rolled over dead.[2]

Eight years later, in 1960, Manning took vows to enter the Franciscan priesthood. One of the requirements upon entering the priesthood was for each priest to take a saint's name as a symbol of his new identity. The year Richard took his vows, priests were allowed to choose their own first names. That's how Richard Manning became Brennan Manning. Someone else's sacrifice had changed the course of his life. And gratitude gave him a new name.

What's the *Story* of This Particular Book?

The Israelites have been wandering around in the desert for almost 40 years at this point; they're no doubt hot, sweaty and beyond exhausted. Plus, they've just buried their beloved leader, Moses. But now they can finally see the light at the end of their trekking tunnel, so they take a deep breath, square their shoulders, pick up the pace and—with Joshua's (their new captain) leadership—make the last push into the Promised Land. Then, following a raucous celebration and a division of "spoils" (see Joshua 13–21), God's people sit back, soak their feet, take stock of their situation and then thank their Creator for all He's done for them over the past four decades (see Joshua 22). After all of the whining and faithlessness and infighting displayed on their arduous journey from Egypt, the Israelites finally display *gratitude*!

Henrietta's Highlights on Joshua

Her Synopsis
Joshua Portrays Jesus Christ, Captain of Our Salvation

Her Suggested Bible Readings
Sunday: *Joshua's Commission* (Joshua 1–2)
Monday: *Crossing the Jordan* (Joshua 3)
Tuesday: *The Fall of Jericho* (Joshua 6)
Wednesday: *The Sin of Achan* (Joshua 7)
Thursday: *Occupation of the Land* (Joshua 11)
Friday: *Caleb's Possession* (Joshua 14)
Saturday: *Joshua's Farewell* (Joshua 24)

Memorable Quotes from Dr. Mears
"Joshua completes what Moses began! God never leaves His work unfinished. Remember the great Craftsman always has another tool sharpened and ready for use."

"So it is in all our work in the world, especially in our Christian service. We are just a part in a mighty whole. Do your little part and do not care if it is not singled out in the completed whole. The waters of the brook are lost in the river."

Looking for Yourself in God's Love Story

1. Read Joshua 7. Achan's seemingly harmless shoplifting caused all of Israel to experience undue pain and anguish (they lost troops in a military defeat due to his disobedience). How is the moral of this story connected to 1 Corinthians 12:12-26 and Ephesians 4:16?

2. Read Joshua 3–4. The Jordan River crossing is reminiscent of the Red Sea miracle at the beginning of the Israelite's journey to the Promised Land. And this time God tells Joshua to build a stone altar—a memorial to His faithfulness—so that future generations will see that pile of rocks and get to hear the story of how Jehovah was with Israel. What are some tangible ways of *remembering God's goodness* with our own friends and family?

Movie Clip Moment

Homeward Bound: The Incredible Journey (1993) is a movie that helps children (or adults with childlike hearts) understand the arduous trip from Egypt to the Promised Land. This adventure film involves three underdressed but likable animals: *Chance*, a frisky bulldog puppy; *Sassy*, a condescending Himalayan cat; and *Shadow*, a wise, aged—very Moses-ish!—Golden Retriever. Their incredible journey home across the rugged Sierra mountain range is very similar to the Israelites' difficult trek to Canaan. Plus, the conclusion brims with gratitude, much like the end of the book of Joshua! This is a great flick that can easily segue into a family devotional.

But for the Grace of God, There Goes Me

Last week a very prominent, well-known pastor resigned from his megachurch amid allegations from a male escort regarding homosexual encounters and methamphetamine use. Of course, this ugly story has already been picked up by the networks, FOX and CNN and has been splashed across the pages of *USA Today*. This pastor's regrettable behavior has made really big news.

By the time you read this devotional, I hope this whole sordid story will be less than a blip on the radar screen of our national consciousness. I've had the privilege of sitting under this particular pastor and found him to be a wonderful Bible teacher. He seemed humble and kind and authentic. He also seemed earnest yesterday when he soberly admitted that some of the allegations were true, and then repented.

But my opinion doesn't mean much. He'll still be the laughingstock of talk radio for the next few weeks. Mean-spirited strangers will rifle through his private life, hoping to find something else to exploit. There will be a voyeuristic feeding frenzy. The mud is already flying. And Pharisees from within the Body of Christ will probably sling more stones than anyone else. It's so much easier to point at someone else's sin and recoil in horror than it is to look in the mirror and say, "He looks a lot like me."

> Amazing grace, how sweet the sound
> That saved a wretch like me!
> I once was lost but now am found,
> Was blind but now I see.

John Newton, ship captain and slave trader turned preacher and hymn writer, captured what should be the attitude of all believers when he penned those lines more than 200 years ago—especially the "wretch like me" part. Mr. Newton didn't pretend to be above reproach. He no doubt remembered the cries of desperate mamas and daddies when he'd separated them from their children and locked them below deck. Although he'd repented and had become an outspoken, courageous advocate for the abolition of slavery, he never forgot the despicable behavior he was capable of.

Scripture makes it crystal clear that we're all capable of really yucky stuff—that we're all born with crooked, polluted hearts. Without the blood Jesus shed on the cross, we're all spiritually filthy, without any hope of being reconciled with our Creator. God help us if we think we're better than our neighbor, that our rebellion is less repugnant than *anyone* else's.

Obviously the Christian leader who's been publicly vilified and humiliated this week made a foolish mistake and turned away from the God he trusts. For a moment or two or three (this pastor ultimately admitted to numerous sexual sins), he chose to follow his lust instead of clinging to the Lover of his soul. And he's paying a very high price for his disobedience: He has lost the church he founded, his career in ministry and his reputation.

I simply refuse to add the jagged-edged rock of judgment to his growing pile of consequences. Plus, I know that tomorrow I could be standing in his shoes. Apart from God's unmerited favor, I'm a mistake-prone woman, prone to wander. The whole point of the gospel is that we're *all* a mess—and in desperate need of a Messiah.

No one is too bad for the grace of Christ, but no one is too good for it either.

What's the *Story* of This Particular Book?

The events recorded in the book of Judges took place at a time in Israel's history when there was no king on the throne, the Word of God wasn't being taught in the land, and everyone was doing what was right in his or her own eyes. Basically it was a recipe for spiritual disaster! God's people had entered the Promised Land, but instead of living lives of devotion and gratitude toward the Lord, they started spiraling out of control. They pointedly ignored His commands and started behaving every bit as badly as the pagans around them.

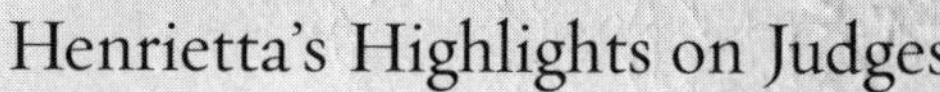

Henrietta's Highlights on Judges

Her Synopsis
Jesus Christ, Our Deliverer Judge

Her Suggested Bible Readings

Sunday: *Only Partial Victories* (Judges 1–2:5)
Monday: *Institution of the Judges* (Judges 2:16–3:11)
Tuesday: *Deborah and Barak* (Judges 4:4-24; 5)
Wednesday: *Gideon, the Farmer* (Judges 6:1-16; 7:13-25)
Thursday: *Jephthah's Terrible Vow* (Judges 11:12-40)
Friday: *Samson, the Strong Man* (Judges 15–16)

Memorable Quotes from Dr. Mears

"The book begins with compromise and ends with confusion."

"One thing we learn in the book of Judges is that a people who spend much of their time in disobedience to God make little progress during their lifetime."

"Human pride would love to believe that humanity's trend is upward. But God's Word shows us that the natural course is downward."

Looking for Yourself in God's Love Story

1. Has someone you knew and respected as a spiritual leader ever fallen into obvious and ugly sin? If so, how did his or her rebellion affect you emotionally?

2. How do Gideon's and Samson's biographies highlight 1 Corinthians 1:26-28 and Hebrews 11:32-34?

3. Read Judges 4:17-22. Does Jael's courage—and creative use of a tent peg—remind you of a brave Christian woman who lives in your corner of the world?

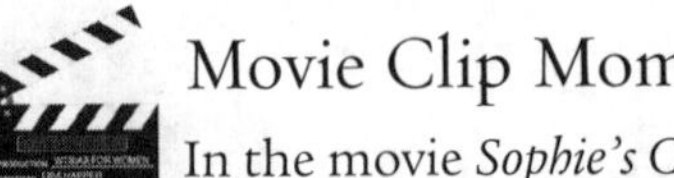

Movie Clip Moment

In the movie *Sophie's Choice*, Meryl Streep portrays a Polish mother who has to make a choice that scars her for the rest of her life. The heart-rending moment takes place when Sophie is standing outside Auschwitz with her two children, a little boy and a little girl, and a sadistic Nazi soldier forces her to make the most difficult decision a parent could ever make. This sad story isn't for the faint of heart, or for children (there are some explicit scenes). But it is a powerful reminder about the depravity humans are capable of apart from God's divine intervention.

Struggling with Sovereignty

Every Mother's Day, a ministry in town sponsors an old-fashioned hymn sing at the Belle Meade Plantation, which is a beautiful old Southern plantation home that's open to the public. It's a wonderful event that includes good food, incredible music, several hundred families and several thousand fireflies. It's a night when Nashville feels more like Mayberry than the big, metropolitan city it's become.

A few years ago (when I lived in a cottage right around the corner from the plantation), I walked over to the hymn sing with a few friends and a comfy folding chair. It was a perfect spring night, complete with balmy temperature and no mosquitoes! And I was thoroughly enjoying myself when reality collided with my heart. I was talking with my friend Carol at the sweet-tea table (told you it was *Southern*!) when a young girl carrying a basket of long-stemmed daisies approached us.

She handed a flower to Carol—who was holding her 18-month-old, chocolate-chip-covered daughter—and sweetly said, "Happy Mother's Day!" Then she turned to me and innocently asked, "Are you a mother?"

I felt like shouting, "No, I don't have a husband, let alone kids—and my heart's ripped in half over it! I didn't even go to church this morning because I didn't want to ruin all my mommy friends' special day by sobbing in the sanctuary, so I just stayed home!"

But I didn't want to traumatize a 10-year-old, so I just smiled and said, "No, I'm not."

Some days I lose sight of the fact that this world is not my home. Some nights I toss and turn because my contentment has affixed itself to what I long for instead of what I already possess. Sometimes the disappointment that comes with unrealized dreams and difficult realities causes me to doubt God's sovereignty.

All the time, He holds me in the midst of my disbelief.

What's the *Story* of This Particular Book?

If anyone had a legitimate reason to doubt God's sovereignty, it was Ruth. Her husband died when she was young; her also-widowed mother-in-law, Naomi, is bitter and grouchy—not exactly the kind of mother-in-law you'd want to go to the mall with. Still, Ruth moves from her cool, metropolitan hometown to a dinky, dusty village (where there's no Starbucks or high-speed Internet) with that same grumpy lady; and the two of them are now so poor she has to grovel for grain just to survive (if you've ever been on Weight Watchers, those scavenged-barley meals are zero points!). But in spite of her difficult circumstances, Ruth—a brand-new believer—doesn't distrust Jehovah's goodness. And the Paul Harvey "rest of the story" points to the fact that God is *always* good, no matter what life throws at you! It also sets in motion the ancestry of Jesus, humanity's Kinsman Redeemer!

Henrietta's Highlights on Ruth

Her Synopsis
Ruth Portrays Jesus Christ, Our Kinsman-Redeemer

Her Suggested Bible Readings
Day One: *The Story of Ruth* (book of Ruth)

Memorable Quote from Dr. Mears
"Ruth was the great-grandmother of David. This book establishes the lineage of David, the ancestor of Christ. It tells of the beginning of the Messianic family within the Messianic nation into which, over a thousand years later, the Messiah was to be born."

Looking for Yourself in God's Love Story

In light of Ruth's story, can you point to a time in your life when God created a treasure out of something that initially seemed tragic?

Movie Clip Moment

I'll admit it, I'm a sucker for sweet animal movies—and the recent *Because of Winn Dixie* is near the top of my list! This film is about a 10-year-old girl, her well-intentioned but oft-flummoxed preacher father, a motley crew of small-town misfits and a shaggy pooch named Winn Dixie. While this story doesn't seem in any way similar to Ruth's at first, by the end you'll definitely see the common theme of redemption. You'll recognize that unique sweetness that grows from sadness. And you'll be reaching for more Kleenex, too!

Learning to Look Outside the Lines

My mom has a special relationship with my brother's son, John Michael. He's her youngest grandchild and the one she spends the most time with because he's the only one who lives nearby (my sister and her family live in another state). Plus, I think he charmed his way into her highest affections by calling her "Onnie" when he was first learning to communicate. His baby talk took awhile to translate, but she eventually realized that it was his own unique version of "honey," which he'd heard Dad call her often!

Anyway, John Michael—who's now seven—and "Onnie" have become two peas in a pod and share lots of hilarious conversations while hanging out together. Mom calls at least once a week with some new anecdote that happened during one of their adventures! She called recently to tell me about his observations on aging.

It went something like this: They were driving to the grocery store, listening to their favorite worship tape (due to Mom's influence, John Michael's an enthusiastic Bill and Gloria Gaither fan!), when he piped up from the backseat to ask, "Hey, Onnie, how old is your mother?"

To which she replied, "She's 94, baby."

A few seconds passed before he asked curiously, "Do you *have* to love people with wrinkles, Onnie?"

So, Mom—always looking for teachable moments with her adorable charge—launched into a Bible lesson about unconditional love. She explained that we weren't supposed to love people simply because we liked how they looked. She drove the message home by describing people who weren't necessarily physically beautiful but who were still worthy of affection. Then—loosely quoting from 1 Samuel—she closed with this climactic statement, "John Michael, people look at the outward appearance but God looks at the heart!"

She said he was absolutely silent, staring out the window for a long moment. Then he took a deep breath and declared with earnest emphasis, "Your mom sure is a good lookin' gal, Onnie!"

What's the *Story* of This Particular Book?

The story of 1 Samuel takes place when the 12 tribes of Israel have settled down into the Promised Land and become much more cohesive. However, although they gelled as a "team," they also succumbed to peer pressure and begged God for a human king in order to be like the pagan nations surrounding them. Jehovah answered their sinful request with a guy named Saul, who proved to be a very regrettable demand! The man who served as Israel's spiritual leader during this season was Samuel. He was the first child born to a godly woman named Hannah (see 1 Samuel 1), whose faithfulness set a great example for her son. Samuel's resume is full of highlights, but the pinnacle of his career in ministry had to be when he anointed a teenager named David—who wasn't necessarily an impressive physical specimen at the time—as God's choice for the next king of Israel (see 1 Samuel 16).

Henrietta's Highlights on 1 Samuel

Her Synopsis
First Samuel Portrays Jesus Christ, Our King

Her Suggested Bible Readings
Sunday: *Samuel, "Name of God"* (1 Samuel 1-3)
Monday: *Samuel, the Prophet* (1 Samuel 4-7)
Tuesday: *Saul, the King* (1 Samuel 8-12)
Wednesday: *Saul, the Self-Willed* (1 Samuel 13-15)
Thursday: *David Anointed* (1 Samuel 16-18)
Friday: *David's Adventures* (1 Samuel 19-20; 22; 24)
Saturday: *Death of Samuel and Saul* (1 Samuel 25-26; 31)

Memorable Quotes from Dr. Mears
"Royal history begins with the book of Samuel. The long period of the rule of the judges ends with Samuel."

"Throughout Samuel's long and useful life he was God's man. He was preeminently a man of prayer."

"In this book we see David as a shepherd lad, a minstrel, an armor bearer, a captain, the king's son-in-law, a writer of psalms and a fugitive."

Looking for Yourself in God's Love Story

1. Did reading about Israel's selfish request for a leader "with skin on" remind you of a time when you begged God for something that you later regretted having asked for?

2. In one of Saul's more obvious missteps, he doesn't have the patience or discipline to wait on God's answer and instead calls the Old Testament version of the "Psychic Hotline" for guidance (see 1 Samuel 28)! What and/or whom do you tend to turn to for wisdom when God seems silent or slow to respond?

3. Because of Saul's pathological jealousy, David spent many years on the run for his life, sometimes literally hiding out in caves (see 1 Samuel 21:10-15; 22). How do you think cooling his heels in caverns helped prepare David to lead Israel?

Movie Clip Moment

I Am Sam is a movie that will work like meat tenderizer on your heart! In this poignant story, the versatile Sean Penn portrays Sam—a mentally challenged man who is raising his young daughter (played by Dakota Fanning) by himself. There are numerous scenes in this film that will bring to mind the words God whispered to Samuel when he was interviewing Jesse's sons for the position of Israel's top dog: "The LORD does not look at the things man looks at. Man looks at the outward appearance, but the LORD looks at the heart" (1 Samuel 16:7).

Limp Toward the One Who Loves You

One of my favorite stories in the Old Testament about God's merciful largess centers around a little boy with a name that's hard to pronounce:

> Jonathan son of Saul had a son who was lame in both feet. He was five years old when the news about Saul and Jonathan came from Jezreel. His nurse picked him up and fled, but as she hurried to leave, he fell and became crippled. His name was Mephibosheth (2 Samuel 4:4).

Mephibosheth was the grandson of Saul, the first king of Israel and David's nemesis. Saul hated David because he was jealous of David—he had even tried to kill David several times. Interestingly enough, Jonathan, who was Saul's oldest son and Mephibosheth's daddy, was also David's best friend. The Bible tells us that Jonathan loved David as much as he loved himself. Because of his affection for his friend, he ultimately defied his father, King Saul, and saved David from certain death when he heard about a plot to kill him.

Years later the Philistines fought against Israel and tried to kill King Saul and his sons so that they could overthrow his kingdom. They killed three of his sons—including Jonathan—and critically wounded Saul. Then Saul took his own sword and killed himself so that he wouldn't be captured by the Philistines.

After many battles between the house of David and the house of Saul, David finally occupied the throne of Israel. In those days, one of the first things a new king did was to kill all of the family members of the previous king (remember the Russian Czar and Anastasia?), thereby getting rid of any potential opposition. Of course, David had no intention of following that tradition, but the few remaining relatives of Saul didn't know that. And they were especially worried about the safety of five-year-old Mephibosheth, because with the deaths of his grandfather, father and uncles, he was the presumptive heir to the throne. So they hurried to escape and that's when the nurse accidentally dropped him. Then they moved to a place called *Lo Debar*, which literally means "barren place."

Twenty years later, there's a knock at Bo's door (surely his friends didn't call him his full name), and a well-dressed official from Jerusalem asks him to gather his things and accompany him to the palace of King David. He's probably terrified, and his fear is legitimate. What would the king want with a cripple, the grandson of the insane Saul who had tried to kill him? I'll bet what happens next is the last thing he expected!

> When Mephibosheth son of Jonathan, the son of Saul, came to David, he bowed down to pay him honor. David said, "Mephibosheth!" "Your servant," he replied. "Don't be afraid," David said to him, "for I will surely show you kindness for the sake of your father Jonathan. I will restore to you all the land that belonged to your grandfather Saul, and you will always eat at my table." And Mephibosheth lived in Jerusalem, because he always ate at the king's table, and he was crippled in both feet (2 Samuel 9:6-7,13).

I have so much in common with Mephibosheth. I've spent most of my life trying to hide the fact that I'm crippled. But no matter how much I try to have all my ducks in a row, no matter how well I perform, I will never, ever be perfect. I'm crippled by insecurity, by the desire to please man sometimes more than God, and by fickle faith. And yet, just like Mephibosheth, the King of kings has called me "daughter" and beckoned me to sit at His banquet table in spite of my deformities.

Hallelujah, what a Savior!

What's the *Story* of This Particular Book?

This book narrates the adult life of David, the shepherd boy who became the king of Israel and one of the most prolific leaders in human history. This divine biography includes many spiritual highs of David's life—his generosity with Bo; his vision of the

Temple (which his son, Solomon, would ultimately build); his numerous military victories over God's enemies; his jubilant jig before the Lord to celebrate the return of the Ark of the Covenant to Jerusalem; and God's promise that Immanuel would come through his lineage. But it also records many missteps that David made as God's number one guy—his unwise choice of wives; his adulterous affair with beautiful Bathsheba; and his murderous scheme to keep her husband, Uriah, in the dark. The overall theme of David's story could be summed up this way: "One Imperfect Man Trying His Best to Love God and Lead God's People."

Henrietta's Highlights on 2 Samuel

Her Synopsis
Second Samuel Portrays Jesus Christ, Our King

Her Suggested Bible Readings

Sunday: *David Mourns for Jonathan and Saul* (2 Samuel 1)
Monday: *David, King of Judah* (2 Samuel 2; 3:1)
Tuesday: *David, King of All Israel* (2 Samuel 5:1-25)
Wednesday: *David's House Established* (2 Samuel 7)
Thursday: *David's Sin* (2 Samuel 11)
Friday: *David's Repentance* (2 Samuel 12:1-23; Psalm 51)
Saturday: *David Numbers the People* (2 Samuel 24:1-17)

Memorable Quotes from Dr. Mears

"The book of 1 Samuel records the failure of the people's king, Saul. Second Samuel describes the enthronement of God's king, David, and the establishment of the 'House of David' through which the Messiah, Jesus Christ, should later come."

"No one found anywhere in God's Word is so versatile. He is David, the shepherd boy, the court musician, the soldier, the true friend, the outcast captain, the king, the great general, the loving father, the poet, the sinner, the brokenhearted old man, but always the lover of God."

"The greatness of your spiritual power is the measure of your surrender. It is not a question of who you are, or of what you are, but whether God controls you."

Looking for Yourself in God's Love Story

1. Read 2 Samuel 12:1-14. Have you ever been approached by a "Nathan," someone who loved you enough to be honest with you about your sin? Have you ever been a "Nathan" to one of your believing friends?

2. Read Psalm 23, one of David's most beloved songs. Summarize David's lyrics in your own words. Describe your most recent being-alone-with-God-in-a-beautiful-place experience.

3. When David danced before the Lord (see 2 Samuel 6:14-16), his grouchy wife, Michal, got really mad. She thought his behavior was absolutely inappropriate. Have you ever had someone accuse you of religious impropriety when you knew your heart was pure before God? If so, how did you respond?

Movie Clip Moment

In my opinion as a ticket buyer and DVD renter, one of the very best movies for your money is *Luther*. This film is based on the life and ministry of Martin Luther (played by Joseph Fiennes), the infamous German monk who infuriated Catholic leadership and kicked off the Protestant Reformation in the sixteenth century through his unwavering commitment to the grace of the gospel. To be sure, this man had flaws, but he was a great leader—determined to honor God to the best of his ability in every thing he did. Luther's devotion reminds me of that of David. This true story is so compelling, so inspirational, that I simply can't choose one particular clip to recommend. You'll just have to watch the whole thing!

Throwing in the Towel

About 10 years ago I bought a small fixer-upper cottage in a nice Nashville neighborhood. With a contractor for a dad, the power of a Home Depot credit card and the enthusiastic willingness to invest sweat equity, I thought we could restore the house and make some money in the process. Little did I know that this "little project" would test my endurance like nothing else!

For example, once when my mom and stepfather, John (who'd also worked as a carpenter in his younger days), came to town for a working visit, we decided to replace a wall-sized window with a pair of French doors, as well as take care of a few leaky bedroom windows. However, after removing the first window, John came down with the flu, leaving a huge 7-by-12-foot hole in the side of the living room, which effectively transformed it into a display case—kind of like those terrariums kids made in elementary school. Folks driving by could entertain themselves simply by observing us through the gaping cavity!

Of course it was the hottest August on record, so to keep my air-conditioning bill below the national deficit, we had to turn the thermostat up to 90 degrees. Half crazed by the heat, humidity and his own fever, John stumbled off the couch the following morning and removed one of the smaller windows in the guest bedroom. But in spite of manual coaxing and many cuss words, he couldn't get the replacement to fit, so he eventually gave up and collapsed back on the couch, leaving another hole in his wake. Meanwhile, I had to drive to the airport to pick up three more houseguests. Did I mention that my cottage has two bedrooms and one bath?

After a few days of rain, coupled with the claustrophobia that came with six people sharing mini-living quarters, I didn't think things could get any worse. But then I wrecked my best friend's Lexus SUV, which I'd borrowed for yet another Home Depot run (for plastic sheeting to plug the gaps where windows had once sat). As I stood there on the side of the road amid the flashing blue lights of three police cars, the curious stares of on-lookers and a very loud ambulance (the woman I tapped made a big fuss about a possible neck injury and demanded medical attention—evidently the victim of too many personal injury lawyer commercials while watching soap operas), I pondered, *I wonder what these policemen would do if I just scurried under that bush over there and started sobbing hysterically?*

When's the last time you felt like crawling under some landscaping and crying?

What's the *Story* of This Particular Book?

The historical narrative of 1 Kings (1 and 2 Kings were combined as one book in the original Hebrew, along with 1 and 2 Samuel and 1 and 2 Chronicles) archives the activities and adventures of the initial rulers of Israel. This royal batting order begins with David's smart yet girl-crazy son, Solomon, who became king after a tug-of-war with his brothers (see 1 Kings 1–2). The entire first half of this book is dedicated to documenting his monarchy. The second half of this literary saga records the decline of Israel's unity as a nation and includes the bios of some pretty crummy kings (see 1 Kings 12–22). Woven throughout the later chapters of 1 Kings (and the beginning of 2 Kings) is a wonderful tale about a prophet named Elijah, who acts as God's champion in one of the most colorful battles between good and evil (see 1 Kings 18). But afterward he runs out of spiritual gas and curls up and cries under a broom tree (see 1 Kings 19). His story is a great reminder that God's goodness endures even when His children give up!

Henrietta's Highlights on 1 Kings

Her Synopsis
First Kings Portrays Jesus Christ as King

Her Suggested Bible Readings
Day One: *Building and Dedicating the Temple* (1 Kings 6:1-14; 8:22-53)
Day Two: *Solomon's Glorious Reign* (1 Kings 10)
Day Three: *The Kingdom Divided* (1 Kings 12)
Day Four: *The Prophet Elijah* (1 Kings 17–18)

Memorable Quotes from Dr. Mears

"Kings begins with King David and ends with the king of Babylon. Kings opens with the building of the Temple and ends with the burning of the Temple."

"Religious apostasy had been gnawing like a deadly worm at the root of Israel's life. One day the tree fell. Nothing destroys a nation like religious decline."

Looking for Yourself in God's Love Story

1. Read 1 Kings 18. Have you ever had a "Mount Carmel" season in your life when everything was going your way and you felt like a champion? If so, what happened when the season ended?

2. Read 1 Kings 19. Who's the meanest, most intimidating "Jezebel" in your life right now? How do you typically respond to her threats and/or insults?

3. How has God tangibly whispered hope amid your curling-up-and-crying moments?

Movie Clip Moment

The movie *Ray* chronicles Ray Charles's real-life journey from a poor, blind little boy to a world-famous musician. There's a poignant scene early in the film when young Ray trips and falls on the floor of the shack he shares with his mama. Her response depicts a loving, protective parent who doesn't turn her back when her child's in trouble but who is also wise enough to let her son learn the painful lessons of endurance and perseverance.

The Greatest Physician of All

My sister, Theresa, and her family are big beach lovers. Fortunately, since they live in Birmingham, the beautiful Gulf of Mexico is just a four or five hour drive. It's not uncommon for Theresa to take off with their two boys (Jordan and Andrew) for the week and then have her husband, James, join them for the weekend. But once—when they were doing just that—something happened that shook my sister to the core—and dramatically affected her prayer life.

She said everything was fine when they began the trip. Jordan was about five at the time and Andrew was just a baby, less than a year old. However, about halfway into their journey Andrew began to howl. He screamed and screamed and she couldn't get him to settle down. She was in the middle of nowhere and didn't know what to do until she finally made it to a small hospital near the shore. She raced into the emergency room with one wide-eyed little boy and another in obvious distress.

Minutes later—before she could catch her breath—a tall physician approached her and soberly asked, "Do you pray for your children?"

She was so flustered by the circumstances and taken aback by his question that she stammered and then replied, "All I've been focusing on is getting my child to a doctor, so I haven't prayed today. But, yes, I usually pray a lot for my children."

To which he responded, "Do you mind if I lay hands on your little boy and pray?" She said she'd appreciate his prayers and watched while he leaned down, placed his hand on her baby's belly and asked God—the *Great* Physician—to heal him.

She later found out that the doctor had recently lost his wife and one of his children in a car accident and was studying to become a priest. She also found out that Andrew's test results revealed his stomach was detached from whatever it was supposed to be attached to and that he was being transferred to a larger hospital for emergency surgery.

Between tearful phone calls to James—who was racing to join them—and the harried trip to the next city, Theresa forgot about the unusual prayer and the curious agent who had prayed it—that is, until the surgeon at the big hospital walked into their room holding new X-ray films and declared, "I'm not sure what happened, but your son's stomach is fine now. He won't be needing surgery after all."

What's the *Story* of This Particular Book?

This book is the seamless continuation of 1 Kings. Although the plot thickens as the nation of Israel is now divided in two distinct regions: Judah, the Southern Kingdom (which included the capital city of Jerusalem and the Temple); and Israel, the Northern Kingdom (which still bore the name with which God had christened His theocracy). God's rebellious children's sorrows increase with the fall of Israel to their vicious opponent, Assyria (see 2 Kings 17:22-23), along with Babylon's crushing defeat of Judah, the exile of its inhabitants and the complete destruction of the Temple. There aren't too many bright spots in this downward historical spiral, but one happens in chapter 2, with the introduction of Elijah's protégé, Elisha, and another happens in chapter 5, when God uses him in an astonishing healing.

Henrietta's Highlights on 2 Kings

Her Synopsis
Second Kings Portrays Jesus Christ as King

Her Suggested Bible Readings

Day One: *Elijah and Elisha* (2 Kings 2:1-22)
Day Two: *The Captivity of Israel* (the Northern Kingdom) (2 Kings 17:7-23)
Day Three: *The Captivity of Judah* (the Southern Kingdom) (2 Kings 25:1-21)

Memorable Quotes from Dr. Mears

"There is a great difference between the fall of Israel and Judah. Israel was scattered throughout the nations for an indefinite period, but God specified the length of Judah's captivity to seventy years."

"God was using even the rulers of foreign nations to work out His plan."

Looking for Yourself in God's Love Story

1. Read 1 Kings 17:17-24 and 2 Kings 4:8-37. What common denominators can you find in these two separate healings that Elijah and Elisha directed?

2. Read 2 Kings 5:1-19. Why do you think Naaman had to dunk himself *seven* times to be healed—why not just once?

3. Read the eye-popping cautionary tale about name-calling in 2 Kings 2:23-25. What's the moral of this story?

Movie Clip Moment

One of my favorite "physician films" with a recurrent theme of hope and healing is *Something the Lord Made*. Much like 2 Kings, the "miracles" in this movie take place against a backdrop of human prejudice and intolerance. (While the Israelites were divided between Northern and Southern Kingdoms, the American culture that's the setting of this film is divided by the color of people's skin). Like many of the other movies I've suggested (and kind of like Lay's potato chips!), I can't pick just one scene. This one's worth watching from beginning to end. Just for fun, make a list of the traits that the character Vivien Thomas (played by Mos Def) and the prophet Elisha have in common.

1 Chronicles

If We Only Knew

When I was in the third grade, I desperately wanted the sparkling white, ten-speed bicycle prominently displayed in our town's J. C. Penney window. I already had a bike—but it was a hand-me-down from my sister, Theresa. It was pretty rusty, plus it had a banana seat, which was totally uncool in my eight-year-old opinion. I began to daydream about the shiny two-wheeler at Penney's: *If mom and dad would buy it for me, I'd be happy for the rest of my life! I'd never ask for anything ever again—even at Christmas!*

What I didn't know was that my parents were having a hard time financially and a pricey bicycle wasn't in the budget at the time. Yet when Mom tried to explain the situation to me, all I could think was that I was going to have to peddle around on Theresa's old rattletrap until I was 30. So I ran away in tears and, for some strange reason, crawled under my parent's bed to pout. A few minutes later, I heard footsteps coming down the hall and then felt the bed shift as Mom sat down on my hiding place. I held my breath—unsure of whether to reveal myself or not.

But then I heard Mom pick up the phone from its cradle and start dialing a number, so I decided to stay put and not interrupt her. And the next thing I heard was Mom's side of a conversation with my aunt Darlene about buying the bike she was no longer using now that she was in college. My heart started beating faster . . . Darlene's bike wasn't brand new, but it was a really cool Raleigh that I knew would evoke stares of admiration from my friends!

I can also remember feeling ashamed as I listened to my mother work out a payment plan with her baby sister. Those few moments of eavesdropping taught me a lot about sacrificial love. In spite of my bratty behavior, Mom still did everything she could to make my dream come true. Her mercy stretched far beyond my self-centeredness.

I wonder what it would be like if we could overhear the conversations God has with His Son about us. My guess is that we'd be absolutely overwhelmed by the extent of His affection.

However, as it is written, "No eye has seen, no ear has heard, no mind has conceived what God has prepared for those who love him" (1 Corinthians 2:9).

What's the *Story* of This Particular Book?

The ancient journal of Chronicles was written soon after the Israelites returned home from their arduous captivity in Babylon (450-430 B.C.). And I think the basic theme of this book could be titled "If They Only Knew," because the author (most historians point to Ezra) compiled the "best of" memories of Israel's walk with God and spliced them together in this literary highlight reel (1 Chronicles is mostly an overview of 1 and 2 Samuel, with David's life story taking up most of the space)—as if reminding God's people of His protection, providence and provision would keep them from spiraling out of spiritual control again.

Henrietta's Highlights on 1 Chronicles

Her Synopsis
First Chronicles Portrays Jesus Christ as King

Her Suggested Bible Readings

Day One: *Bringing the Ark Home to Jerusalem* (1 Chronicles 13; 15:25-39)
Day Two: *David's Psalm of Thanks* (1 Chronicles 16:7-36)
Day Three: *Preparations for the Temple* (1 Chronicles 28)

Memorable Quote from Dr. Mears
"Through such books as the Chronicles we get the history of the Jewish nation. Through this nation our Lord came to earth."

Looking for Yourself in God's Love Story

Read 1 Chronicles 10:13-14. Why do you think the chronicler vilified Saul for his *spiritual* adultery, yet chose to omit the story of his successor's (King David) sexual adultery?

Movie Clip Moment

When I think of the best film example of a chronicler, Michael Keaton (playing Bob Jones) in *My Life* comes quickly to mind. Bob is a hardworking guy who gets the great news that his wife, Gail (Nicole Kidman), is going to have their first child–about the same time he receives the tragic news that he's dying of cancer and won't be around to watch their baby grow up. Bob decides to videotape himself, thereby leaving behind a diary of love (along with some humorous Technicolor tutoring lessons) for his son. Near the beginning of this emotionally evocative movie, there's a clip that explains the heart and soul of a chronicler.

The Faintest Trace of Family Resemblance

My friend Dolly has three girls, Libby, Cindy and Julie—none of whom bears much resemblance to their mother when it comes to personality. Dolly is mild-mannered, her daughters are spunky; she plays by the rules, they push the envelope; she seeks the slow life in the country, they savor cavorting in the city. They're all adults now, but they definitely kept Dolly on her toes when they were little!

She recently told me a story about a shopping spree that went awry with her frisky offspring. Hardy (Dolly's husband and the trio's dad) had taken her and the girls with him on a business trip with plans of family fun after his conference was over. The only catch was that Dolly would have to keep the girls occupied until he could join them. After exhausting the hotel pool and in-room movie menu, she packed everyone off to a nearby mall.

Though they were in a strange city, Dolly gave in to their request to shop by themselves. She reasoned that they were mature enough to be unsupervised, plus she found herself longing for a bit of alone time, too. After planning a time and place to meet, Dolly and her daughters went their separate ways. An hour or so later, Dolly was strolling along when she noticed a blind woman and her solicitous companion coming toward her. She thought what a perfect pair they made, as she watched the sighted woman gracefully guide her handicapped friend out of harm's way.

But as the couple got closer, Dolly found herself staring at two of the stinkers she'd given birth to! Cindy was playing the part of dignified groper, while Julie—playing the part of caring attendant—steered her slowly down the corridor. Of course, both burst into giggles when they approached their mortified mama! And Dolly put her thespian skills to the test by pretending not to know the politically incorrect delinquents!

If God were a human parent, He'd surely be regularly redfaced as a result of our inappropriate behavior. If He weren't supernaturally patient, surely He'd turn around and pretend not to know us. As apples, we've fallen a very long way from our paternal tree!

What's the *Story* of This Particular Book?

This book is the sequel to 1 Chronicles, a culmination of Israel's "sacred" history—which often appears more insubordinate than sacred! And whereas the first book focused mostly on David, this one shifts to the life of his son, Solomon; the kings that succeeded him; and several spiritual revivals that rekindled Israel's love for God (synopsizing the material recorded in 1 and 2 Kings).

Henrietta's Highlights on 2 Chronicles

Her Synopsis
Chronicles Portrays Jesus Christ as King

Her Suggested Bible Readings
Day One: *Asa* (2 Chronicles 15)
Day Two: *Jehoshaphat* (2 Chronicles 20)
Day Three: *Joash* (2 Chronicles 23–24)
Day Four: *Hezekiah* (2 Chronicles 29–31)
Day Five: *Josiah* (2 Chronicles 35)

Memorable Quote from Dr. Mears
"Jesus Christ is portrayed as King in the books of Kings and Chronicles."

Looking for Yourself in God's Love Story

Read 2 Chronicles 4 and 5, along with 1 Corinthians 3:16 and 2 Corinthians 6:16. How do you think the glorious opulence of God's literal Temple in Jerusalem can be reflected in us?

Movie Clip Moment

There's a quietly compelling scene in the film *The Shawshank Redemption* in which Morgan Freeman (playing a wizened old convict) explains the impact incarceration can have on a man's psyche. He says, "These walls, at first you hate 'em. Then you get used to 'em. And after a while, you find out that you need 'em." It's a powerful statement about how oppression and confinement numb your soul. And while I certainly don't recommend this gritty flick for kids, I do think adults can learn a lot about the probable disposition of God's people after they returned from their prison term in Babylon (which is the timeframe of 2 Chronicles).

One Sandwich Short of a Happy Meal

My friend Teresa told me another story about a recent interaction that her veterinarian pal, Dr. Peerman, had with one of his more colorful clients. He got a phone call one afternoon from a woman—whom we'll nickname "Flighty" for reasons that will soon be obvious—asking for his advice regarding a sick kitten. Flighty lamented to Dr. Peerman that her little cat was getting weaker and weaker and she didn't know what to do. (Of course, the obvious course of action would have been to bring the animal to the vet's office and actually pay for his help, but evidently Flighty was a tightwad, too!)

Still Dr. Peerman listened patiently as she tearfully listed her pet's symptoms. When she finished the emotive monologue, he gently asked what she'd been feeding her ailing feline. She said they were only giving her milk. Dr. Peerman explained that a kitten's stomach is sometimes too sensitive for cow's milk because it lacks the enzymes to break it down. He went on to describe an alternative milk product that she could purchase at a nearby pet store.

There was a long pause on the other end of the phone and then Flighty said earnestly, "Well, Dr. Peerman, I don't know much about cow milk—we've just been giving this cat the *people* milk that we get down at the grocery store."

What's the *Story* of This Particular Book?

If you aren't familiar with the history of the Israelites, their behavior as recorded in the book of Ezra might come across as a bit flighty, too! Their response when the foundation for the new Temple is laid includes both joyful celebration and loud sobbing. They're laughing and crying, giggling and sniffing. So what's the deal? Are these seemingly confused Hebrews happy or sad? Well, they're both. They're delighted to be back home, away from the oppression of Babylon, and glad to be on the construction team for a new Temple. But they're also in mourning. The older Israelites weep as they realize the consequences of their spiritual disobedience when comparing the current, rather dinky Temple with their previous, much more glorious place of worship. They become conscious of the fact that their rebellion against Jehovah has resulted in severe penalties.

Henrietta's Highlights on Ezra

Her Synopsis

Ezra Portrays Jesus Christ, Our Restorer

Her Suggested Bible Readings

Sunday: *Jews Return to Jerusalem* (Ezra 1–3)
Monday: *Discouragement and Joy* (Ezra 4–6)
Tuesday: *Ezra's Expedition* (Ezra 7–10)
Wednesday: *A Struggle* (Romans 7)
Thursday: *The Life of Victory* (Romans 8)
Friday: *The Jews Set Aside* (Romans 9:30–11:12)
Saturday: *The Christian's Service* (Romans 12)

Memorable Quote from Dr. Mears

"Ezra was the Thomas Jefferson of his time, laying the constitutional foundations for the future. To him we are indebted for codifying Israel's laws and the formation of her Scripture canon."

Looking for Yourself in God's Love Story

1. Read Ezra 9–10. How would you describe the role that *confessing sin* played in Israel's restoration as a nation?

2. Read 1 John 1:9. How would you describe the role confessing sin plays in your sense of personal well-being—feeling whole, peaceful and content?

Movie Clip Moment

October Sky (1999) is a movie about building something important—not as important as the Temple construction project in Ezra, but significant nonetheless! The film, based on a true story, opens in the 1950s mining town of Coalwood, where we meet Homer Hickam (played by Jake Gyllenhaal), a bright young man who's destined to end up working in the local coalmine like his dad. However, in October 1957 when Russia launches Sputnik, the first artificial satellite to orbit in space, boys all over the world are inspired to try to build rockets—including Homer. Of course, lots of people (including his gruff father) think Homer's acting like an idiot—like he's one sandwich short of a Happy Meal. And you'll just have to watch the movie to find out whether or not they're right!

Well Worth the Work

My dear friend Eva Whittington Self was paralyzed in a car accident when she was a senior in high school. When she finally came home from the rehab hospital, she'd learned most of the basic life skills she needed to function from a wheelchair, but there were still a few things she couldn't do by herself—like putting her bluejeans on.

One morning a few days after she'd arrived at home, her mother, May Bell, said she thought it'd be a good day for Eva to learn how to put on her pants by herself. Eva told her mom that'd she'd eventually attempt that, but it was still too hard to manage alone, especially since she'd have to pull them up over a big, bulky back brace. However, Mary Bell—usually a timid, tenderhearted woman—insisted that Eva put her jeans on by herself. After arguing about it, Eva got mad and ordered her mom out of her room. Before she left, Mary Bell carefully stretched the jeans out on the bed so that they would be within Eva's reach.

Eva said she was furious when her mom left, but after fuming awhile, she leaned down and grabbed her jeans by the waistband. It took about 10 minutes to work them up to her knees. Then she threw herself back on the bed, angry and exhausted, and sobbed. After a few minutes she leaned forward again and continued working the pants up. Another 10 or 15 minutes passed, and she was able to work the pants up to her hips. Breathing hard, she fell back on the bed and started crying again. After another short pity party, she took a deep breath and started inching the waistband over the cumbersome plastic back brace.

It took Eva more than half an hour, but she finally got her pants all the way up and buttoned. Then—wet with perspiration—she fell back on the bed a third time. And that was when she heard her mother crying.

May Bell had been in the next room the whole time. It must have broken her heart to listen to Eva struggle, but she loved her too much to let her take the easy way out. She knew that her daughter's path to independence would demand a lot of hard work, and sometimes even pain. In much the same way, our heavenly Father loves us way too much to segregate us from blood, sweat and tears, from things that teach us and stretch us and mold us into much better people.

What's the *Story* of This Particular Book?

Ezra and Nehemiah were originally compiled as one book in the Hebrew Bible and the prophet Ezra wrote this book as well, using information from Nehemiah's journal. Like Ezra, there's both joy and sorrow in this storyline as God's people have come home (from captivity in Babylon), but the home they returned to is a lamentable mess. Under Nehemiah's inspirational leadership, they finally get busy on the long-overdue project of rebuilding the walls around Jerusalem (so as to protect themselves from future bullies). It's really hard, dirty, sweaty, I-think-I've-got-a-herniated-disc kind of work, but their labor of love pays off with a fancy new barrier *and* a huge national revival (see Nehemiah 9).

Henrietta's Highlights on Nehemiah

Her Synopsis
Nehemiah Portrays Jesus Christ, Our Restorer

Her Suggested Bible Readings
Day One: *Nehemiah Rebuilds the Wall* (Nehemiah 1–3)
Day Two: *Overcoming Opposition* (Nehemiah 4–6)
Day Three: *Nehemiah Rebuilds the Morals* (Nehemiah 7–9)
Day Four: *Reforming Through Religion* (Nehemiah 11–13)

Memorable Quote from Dr. Mears
"The Jews had been back home for almost a hundred years, but had made no attempt to build Jerusalem beyond the restoration of the Temple, because their enemies made it almost impossible."

Looking for Yourself in God's Love Story

1. Read Nehemiah 2:1. Nehemiah had a pretty important, pretty cushy job as King Artaxerxes's (Esther's stepson) cupbearer—essentially a trusted assistant. His position afforded him access to cool cars, five-star hotels and gourmet meals. But he gave it all up to go home and do God's work. What have you "given up" so as to serve God better?

2. Read Nehemiah 9. Have you ever been to a modern "revival"—like a Billy Graham crusade or a Women of Faith conference? If so, how did it affect you?

Movie Clip Moment

Life as a House (2001) is a sad but ultimately inspirational film about a man named George who dreams about building a house by the sea, but he puts his dream on a shelf for so long it seems to have evaporated, along with everything else that was once good about his life. When he finally decides to put some elbow grease into his fantasy, nobody—not one family member, friend or neighbor—is interested in raising a hammer to help him. In that way, George (played by Kevin Kline) reminds me of Nehemiah at the beginning of his "Let's Rebuild the Barrier" campaign when the Israelites were reluctant to put on the hard hats he offered. And as with Nehemiah, George's construction project ends up being about much more than bricks and mortar.

A Beautiful (but Unconventional) Bride

My friend Victor Farragalli is Italian through and through and has some wonderful stories about his colorful heritage. One of my favorites stars his grandfather, Vito Colucci, who grew up in Italy but then left for America with his father when he was 14 years old. The plan was for them to sail to the United States, work hard and save money for a few years, then sail back to Italy with bulging bank accounts. And while everyone agreed their sacrifice was necessary for the family's financial survival, Vito's mama wasn't at all happy about saying goodbye to her oldest son. Victor said his grandfather's last memory of his mother—experienced from the railing of the departing ship—was that of her running frantically down the pier after the ocean liner, screaming his name, and then falling onto the dock in a dead faint!

After Vito had been in America for a while, his immigrant friends decided it was time for him to marry a nice girl from the "old country." So they told him about a wonderful girl named Louisa, also from a small village in Italy, who worked in a chicken factory. A day and time was arranged for them to meet and Vito sauntered over to the back entrance of Louisa's workplace. Moments later a dark-haired girl in a white apron came outside. Grandpa Vito said, "I counna believe—she wazza covahed inna blooda! There wazza blooda alla ovah! But then I decida, 'She looka okay.' So I saida, 'Okay, I'lla marry herra.'" Soon after their introduction, Vito Colucci and Louisa Moreno became *manna anna wifa*, and their unconventional marriage lasted for more than 50 years.

It just goes to show that great beauty and true love can be found off the beaten path!

What's the *Story* of This Particular Book?

Esther was certainly not a conventional potential bride for the Persian king Xerxes, who was hunting for a new honey after firing his first wife for insubordination. Esther was an unlikely candidate because she was Jewish. Furthermore, she had been raised by her cousin Mordecai, which probably meant she didn't attend too many debutante balls or have her name inscribed on the "Elite and Available Young Women" list. However, Esther was absolutely beautiful on the outside *and* on the inside, which is ultimately what enabled her to beat out all the other queen wannabes vying for Xerses's attention. Once she was officially chosen as the monarch's new mate, her wisdom and courage helped rescue the entire Jewish nation from annihilation. God used an atypical young newlywed—providentially paired with a human king for "such a time as this"—to save His people from their enemies. This engaging book is part love story, part adventure movie!

Henrietta's Highlights on Esther

Her Synopsis
Esther Portrays Jesus Christ, Our Advocate

Her Suggested Bible Readings
Sunday: *Rejection of Vashti* (Esther 1)
Monday: *Crowning of Esther* (Esther 2)
Tuesday: *Plotting of Haman* (Esther 3–4)
Wednesday: *Venture of Esther* (Esther 5)
Thursday: *Mordecai Exalted* (Esther 6)
Friday: *Esther's Feast* (Esther 7–8)
Saturday: *Deliverance of the Jews* (Esther 9–10)

Memorable Quotes from Dr. Mears
"Esther is like Joseph and David. God had each one hidden away for His purpose. When the day came, He brought them to the front to work out His plan."

"This book of Esther is an important link in a chain of events that tell of reestablishing the Hebrew nation in their own land in preparation for the coming of the Messiah into the world."

Looking for Yourself in God's Love Story

1. Esther and Ruth are the only books in the Bible named after women. What other similarities do you see in their stories?

2. Read Esther 4. Much like Moses at the burning bush, Esther initially wavers when Mordecai tells her she needs to step up to the plate. She's only human and she's afraid. But when Mordecai says, "And who knows but that you have come to royal position for such a time as this?" (Esther 4:14), Esther recognizes her responsibility, takes a deep breath, squares her slim shoulders and walks bravely into a very scary situation. Have you ever experienced a comparable "For Such a Time as This" crossroads where you had to choose between safety and danger, cowardice and courage?

Movie Clip Moment

I think most of the theology espoused in films is about as valuable as doctrine emblazoned on bumper stickers—neither is very trustworthy! But if we're intentional about looking for the redemptive message in movies, there are certainly some worthwhile cinematic moments, such as the Esther-like message of "do something that matters—even if it's painful—for the people you love" in the heart-warming flick *Saint Ralph* (2004). Much of young Ralph's rigid, works-oriented theology is obviously flawed, but you'll still find yourself rooting for this sincere, skinny kid as he races in the Boston Marathon in a courageous effort to "heal" his comatose mother.

No Matter What

My friend Jim was called to the hospital a few years ago to visit Don, a man who'd been in a tragic accident. Don's teenaged daughter had unintentionally backed over him while he was working on the family car, leaving him paralyzed from the neck down. Jim said he was taken aback when he walked into the hospital room and saw Don for the first time. A stainless steel "halo" was fastened to his shaved head with long screws. Tubes and wires monitoring his vital signs sprouted from his shrunken frame. His skin was pale and his breathing was shallow.

Jim said he did his best to make small talk but felt uncomfortable and inadequate. What in the world could he say to encourage a man who'd never move anything but the muscles in his face again? How could he inspire a man who'd seemingly lost everything? Jim said that after a few minutes of fidgeting, the only thing he could think of to do was pray. So he asked Don if it'd be okay for him to pray. Don whispered yes and then asked Jim to come close to the bed so that he could see his face.

Don looked directly into Jim's eyes and said, "Jim, I want you to know that I believe God's sovereignty will *never* take me to a place were His grace can't sustain me." He told Jim that even though he'd never stand again or hug his wife or walk his daughter down the aisle, he knew with all his heart that God still loved him. His quiet but confident voice rose above the hum of the machines sustaining his broken body as he talked about God's goodness in spite of his circumstances.

Don's story—and countless others like his—point to the truth that our heavenly Father's compassion for us will *never* fade or fail, no matter what painful realities we face in this world.

What's the *Story* of This Particular Book?

This familiar saga was written sometime during Moses' and Ezra's eras by an unknown author. The two main themes covered in this book are: *If God is such a good God, why does He allow suffering in His world?* and *How should God's people respond when they have to deal with pain and hardship?* Job—the main character—wrestles with these questions until he gets so frustrated that he demands an audience with God. But then he learns to submit to God's sovereignty after the Creator puts things in perspective by asking a few humbling questions of His own, such as "Where were you when I laid the earth's foundation?" and "Have you ever given orders to the morning, or shown the dawn its place?" (Job 38:4,11).

Henrietta's Highlights on Job

Her Synopsis
Job Portrays Jesus Christ, My Redeemer

Her Suggested Bible Readings
Sunday: *Satan and Saint* (Job 1–2)
Monday: *Bildad Thinks Job a Hypocrite* (Job 8)
Tuesday: *Job Answers His Friends* (Job 12)
Wednesday: *Job's Faith* (Job 19)
Thursday: *Job and Elihu* (Job 32; 37:23-24)
Friday: *God Speaks to Job* (Job 38:1-18)
Saturday: *Job Vindicated and Honored* (Job 42)

Memorable Quotes from Dr. Mears
"Job's key word is 'tried' . . . Trials and suffering are for our education and training. The athlete is not put under strict discipline for punishment, but merely to make him ready for the race."

"God kept dealing with Job till he came to the very end of himself!"

"Only pure gold can stand the fire. All dross is burned up. God, the great metallurgist of heaven, puts us in the fire, but He watches and tries us Himself. He trusts no other. When the fire has burned long enough to destroy the impurities, He pulls us out."

Looking for Yourself in God's Love Story

1. Read John 9:1-3 and Job 1:6-12. Contrast the disciple's misunderstanding of human suffering with God's purpose in hardship.

2. The Bible makes it clear that pain and difficulty fall into three basic categories: (1) the reality of living in a fallen world where "rain" falls on the just and the unjust (see Matthew 5:45); (2) the consequences of sinful choices—of reaping what we sow (see Galatians 6:7); and/or (3) a sign of God's "sifting" (see Malachi 3:1-3). Into which of these categories does most of your suffering seem to fall?

Movie Clip Moment

I Am David is a beautiful story about a little boy who epitomizes undeserved suffering and the motley crew who become his unofficial foster family. By the end of the movie (which is a family-friendly film), you'll see the overarching theme of redemption: how hardship can work like fertilizer on the human heart and how soulful beauty really can come from emotional soot and ashes!

Songs for the Soul

My best friend is a single mom with two boys, Graham and Benjamin, and recently I got to keep the guys at my house while she was out of town. I usually have pretty grandiose plans of how amazing our time together will be—we'll ride bikes and roast marshmallows and read the classics together, but it never quite plays out the way I romanticize being mom-for-a-day will be.

First of all, they're boys with lots of extra energy and a talent for making messes. Plus, I'm learning that boys tend to be tactile—they feel the need to touch, squeeze, poke or punch everything they walk past. Including glass vases, one-of-a kind knickknacks, faux-painted walls and, well, the list goes on. Suffice it to say that within just a few hours in my little cottage, Graham had put chewing gum in the guest room toilet, Benji had spilled ketchup on the dining room rug and one of them accidentally dumped a box of Raisinettes between the cushions of my new leather couch!

I went to bed thinking, *Gosh, this mom thing is hard.* The next day was Sunday, so I assumed peace would reign on our motley crew. However, after church—after Benji had climbed through the doggie door, terrorized my Jack Russell terriers and danced upon my Hydrangeas—I lost it and said a cuss word. Very loudly.

It wasn't a *really* bad word mind you; it was the one that also describes massive concrete structures that retain large bodies of water. But it still stopped Benji dead in his tracks. He looked up at me with big eyes, surprise obvious on his darling, little-boy face, and I thought, *Doggone it, he's going to be in counseling 20 years from now because I've just scarred him for life!* I couldn't believe I'd belted out an expletive immediately after singing hymns and hearing a great sermon. Yikes, talk about being *prone to wander*!

The stuff that leaks out of my heart and mouth is often a tangible indication of why I need Jesus. I'm a fantastically flawed woman, desperate for God's grace and mercy, which is one of the main reasons the psalms resonate with me. These Old Testament lyrics—all originally composed as songs—reveal our utter humanity. They are a powerful reminder that our heavenly Father created real people, with real issues, living in a real world. Some days we'll feel like praising God and some days we'll feel like pouting—but glory to God, who sent a flesh-and-blood Savior to redeem us from our own polluted hearts and from this broken planet.

As the psalmist so eloquently sang, "And I—in righteousness I will see your face; when I awake, I will be satisfied with seeing your likeness" (Psalm 17:15). In other words, when we look into the face of Jesus in a place where there will be no more crying and no more dying, we will be perfectly content.

What's the *Story* of This Particular Book?

The main purpose of the psalms is to give praise to God, but the lyrics also read like a diary of humankind's experience with the Creator and all that He created. These divine songs portray delight and disappointment, awed reverence and humble repentance. They record the dancing and weeping of God's people. They share the roller-coaster ride of our redemption story. Church father John Calvin said it well when he said the psalms provide an "anatomy of all parts of the soul."

They are formally classified into several categories, including: *wisdom* psalms, *penitential* psalms; *royal,* or *Messianic,* psalms; *thanksgiving* psalms; *imprecatory* psalms; psalms of *ascent,* or *pilgrimage*; and the psalms of *lament*. They were written by numerous songwriters, including: David (73 of the 150 are attributed to him); his son Solomon; Asaph (David's "worship leader"); the sons of Korah; Moses; some guy named Ethan; and quite a few are officially listed as anonymous (sometimes referred to as the "orphan" psalms). Ultimately there is a psalm for every circumstance in which we find ourselves!

Henrietta's Highlights on Psalms

Her Synopsis
Psalms Portrays Jesus Christ, Our All in All

Her Suggested Bible Readings
Sunday: *Psalms of Law* (Psalms 1; 19)
Monday: *Psalms of Creation* (Psalms 29; 104)
Tuesday: *Psalms of Judgment* (Psalms 52–53)
Wednesday: *Psalms of Christ* (Psalms 22; 40–41)
Thursday: *Psalms of Life* (Psalms 3; 31)
Friday: *Psalms of the Heart* (Psalms 37; 42)
Saturday: *Psalms of God* (Psalms 90; 139)

Memorable Quotes from Dr. Mears
"No doubt Psalms is the best-loved book in the Old Testament. Someone has called it the solid gold of the Christian experience. Slip in wherever you will and you will find a treasure. Every Psalm is a direct expression of the soul's consciousness of God."

"The Hebrew title of this book is 'Praise,' or the 'Book of Praises,' which indicates that the main contents of the book are praise, prayer and worship."

"They are of God for you. Sing them and make them your own. Catch David's note and spirit. He wrote marching songs, prayer songs, rally songs, hilltop songs, confession songs. Sing as you march. Keep step with David and David's Lord all the way."

Looking for Yourself in God's Love Story

1. Read Psalm 139 and personalize it, inserting your name every time the word "me" appears. What emotions does this song evoke in you?

2. Read Psalm 63. What titles would you use to describe the distinct themes in verses 1-5, verses 6-8 and verses 9-11?

3. It's been said that there can be no worship without wilderness, no praise without pain. Read Psalm 51—David's heart wrenching cry for God's forgiveness—and describe a similar season in your life, a time when you were hiking through a wilderness, feeling distant from your heavenly Father, desperate for His restoration.

Movie Clip Moment

The film *Big Fish*—featuring talented actors like Albert Finney, Jessica Lange and Helena Bonham Carter—paints the picture of a very flawed father and his disillusioned adult son. The son returns to his childhood home to reconnect with his dad, who's dying. It's a poignant, often whimsical, portrayal of his journey to accept his father's flaws and appreciate his father's gifts. *Big Fish* is a beautiful story about having compassion for the mistake-prone people we rub shoulders with. And while this isn't a "Christian" film, there is a bit of Bible trivia in one scene—look for the verse on the message board inside the bank that Winslow robs!

Grinning Because of God

I was speaking at a Christian retreat in Washington, D.C., recently and a woman came rushing up at the end of one of the sessions to exclaim, "You have changed my friend Becky's life! God used your teaching to totally transform her!" She went on to ask if I'd mind talking to Becky for a few minutes, to which of course I said yes. I mean, *good night*, I had changed her life and all!

While the chatty woman was off collecting her "new and improved" companion, I found myself wondering what the story really was. I wondered if Becky had been addicted to drugs. Maybe she was one of those minivan-driving moms who got hooked on methamphetamine while trying to lose a few pounds. Or perhaps she'd been a prostitute with fishnet hose and a little black book hidden in the back of her closet in suburban Virginia. Or what if Becky was a secret agent who'd killed people while engaging in covert government plots—which seemed *almost* plausible, given that the event was taking place a few miles from the Pentagon!

My imagination ran wild thinking about what in the world this chick had been redeemed from.

Then Becky approached. She certainly didn't look like an addict or a spy. She looked like a regular girl. She smiled sheepishly and said, "I just wanted you to know that this is the first time I've ever laughed in a setting that had something to do with God." I thought, *All this fuss was about her giggling with some girlfriends at a retreat?* But then she went on to earnestly explain how she'd been raised in a very rigid church and had been taught that a big part of being a Christian was to be sober-minded. That grinning—much less laughter—was considered completely inappropriate in relation to God. She said the humor we'd experienced throughout the weekend had lifted a huge burden from her shoulders. She was learning to actually *express* the joy of her salvation, the deep sense of delight that comes with trusting in Jesus.

And in that moment, I realized that Becky's makeover from a spiritual scrooge to a mirth-filled mama was a very big deal, because joy is one of the features that distinguish Christians from the rest of the world: the ability to smile—regardless of the situation in which we find ourselves—because we believe that no matter what happens, God is in control, and that whatever He allows to filter into our lives will ultimately work out for our good and His glory, which is undoubtedly why the wise woman in Proverbs had a twinkle in her eye: "She is clothed with strength and dignity; she can laugh at the days to come" (Proverbs 31:25).

What's the *Story* of This Particular Book?

Proverbs is commonly referred to as a "wisdom" book because of the short, wise sayings woven throughout its 31 chapters. One scholar said Proverbs was like a biblical multi-vitamin—he said we should read one every day! Most—if not all—of these proverbs were penned by King Solomon (David's smart son, the third king of Israel), in an effort to tutor some of his favorite students in the things that really matter. The two main themes running through this book are *wisdom* and *foolishness*; wisdom comes from walking with God (see Proverbs 1:7) and foolishness happens when people follow their own selfish path (see Proverbs 1:28-33).

Henrietta's Highlights on Proverbs

Her Synopsis
Jesus Christ, Our Wisdom

Her Suggested Bible Readings
Day One: *Get Wisdom* (Proverbs 1-4)
Day Two: *To Sons* (Proverbs 5-7)
Day Three: *Good and Bad* (Proverbs 15-17)
Day Four: *Wise Words* (Proverbs 20; 22; 31)

Memorable Quotes from Dr. Mears
"In Psalms we find Christians on their knees. In Proverbs we find Christians on their feet. The Psalms are for the Christian's devotions. The Proverbs are for the Christian's walk. The Psalms are for

the closet of prayer. The Proverbs are for the business place, home and playground."

"The book of Proverbs takes us out in the court of the congregation where the people are . . . this is a book for everyday instruction."

"Proverbs is an intensely practical book, exposing a series of traps that would ensnare us."

Looking for Yourself in God's Love Story

1. Read Proverbs 11:22 and 31:30. What do you think these proverbs say about the outward appearance and inward character of women? How do you think God would describe an attractive woman?

2. How would you differentiate between the true wisdom illustrated in Proverbs and worldly "wisdom"?

3. Compare and contrast a biblical *promise* and a biblical *proverb*. Do you think the Proverbs should be applied in every case, regardless of circumstance? Why or why not?

Movie Clip Moment

It's a Wonderful Life, one of the best-loved Christmas films of all times, plays out like one long proverb! Jimmy Stewart is convincing as a down-on-his-luck banker, George Bailey. And while watching him learn some very important life lessons about humility and gratitude (via a colorful angel character named Clarence Oddbody), you'll probably pick up a few pointers yourself. Although the "proverbs" preached in *It's a Wonderful Life* aren't always theologically accurate, there is a pivotal scene in which George calls on the name of God and graces takes place onscreen. But be forewarned, watching this movie might cause dreams about dancing sugarplums—so don't rent it in July!

A Season for Stillness

About 10 years ago, a friend set me up on a blind date with an enthusiastic gentleman whom we'll call "Bob." Following that date, Bob was relentless in his pursuit of me. He sent flowers, wrote letters and sang songs on my answering machine to communicate his affection. Although my response to his overtures wasn't always positive, he was determined to win my affection. Shakespeare would've been proud—Bob pitched some serious woo.

Woo (woo) *transitive verb*: to try to get the love of; to court

Of course, my old beau's passion pales significantly next to that of the Lover of our souls. God's perfect countenance splits into a grin, like a young bridegroom (see Isaiah 62:5), when He sees us coming. He courts us with living letters describing His great love for us (see Romans 15:4). And He serenades us with songs of delight and deliverance (see Zephaniah 3:17). We should rejoice with wonder at being romanced by the Lord of the Universe!

However, I've discovered I'm not very good at being wooed. I have a hard time enjoying God's gifts, savoring the sweetness of His letters and paying attention while His love songs wash over my soul. I'm performance-oriented and my personality leans toward having way too many irons in the proverbial fire, resulting in chaotic busyness. The constant static and activity of my life make lingering and listening difficult, leaving me a weak "wooee." I've only recently begun to practice the discipline of *resting* so that my heart will be pliant for His pursuit.

As His beloved but busy daughters, we must learn that our souls require rest. In order to really respond to our Creator's wooing, we have to be willing to surrender our busyness for a little while. A seventeenth-century French Archbishop named Fénelon wrote with incredible insight about our need to be still, long before drive-thrus and cell phones added to an already chaotic culture: "When it comes to accomplishing things for God, you will find that high aspirations, enthusiastic feelings, careful planning and being able to express yourself well are not worth very much. The important thing is absolute surrender to God."

I'm still in kindergarten when it comes to understanding the concept of absolute surrender, especially giving in to rest. But I'm learning to admit that sometimes I need a nap in order for the posture of my heart to be pleasing to God. I'm also learning that there are seasons when I desperately need to stop *doing* and simply collapse in His embrace.

"There is a time for everything, and a season for every activity under heaven . . . a time to embrace and a time to refrain . . . a time to be silent and a time to speak" (Ecclesiastes 3:1,5,7).

What's the *Story* of This Particular Book?

The name of this book—Ecclesiastes—means "preacher," and most Bible scholars agree that Solomon wrote this sober sermon, especially in light of how the text begins (see Ecclesiastes 1:1). The intended audience appears to be the people of Israel, and the preacher's intention seems to be facilitating a giant coffee chat—because this wise sage ponders some pretty big philosophical questions here. And they don't all end with easy answers! The most familiar passage in Ecclesiastes is the time-for-everything message in chapter 3, but the two overarching themes of this Old Testament scroll are that *the human mind is way too small to comprehend the totality of God* and that *life—apart from God—is one long grind.*

Henrietta's Highlights on Ecclesiastes

Her Synopsis
Jesus Christ, the End of All Living

Her Suggested Bible Readings
Day One: *All Is Vanity* (Ecclesiastes 1–3)
Day Two: *Only God Satisfies* (Ecclesiastes 11–12)

Memorable Quotes from Dr. Mears

"Jesus is the beginning of all in Proverbs. He is the end of all in Ecclesiastes, the 'summum bonum' of life. Wisdom in Proverbs is piety. Wisdom in Ecclesiastes is prudence and sagacity."

"The problem that faced Solomon was how he could find happiness and satisfaction apart from God (Ecclesiastes 1:1-3). He sought satisfaction in science (Ecclesiastes 1:4-11), but could get no answer. He sought it in philosophy (Ecclesiastes 1:12-18), but in vain; he found pleasure (Ecclesiastes 2:1-11), mirth (Ecclesiastes 2:1), drinking (Ecclesiastes 2:3), building (Ecclesiastes 2:4), possession (Ecclesiastes 2:5-7), wealth and music (Ecclesiastes 2:8) all empty."

"We find in this book that we can never find satisfaction and happiness in this world. True happiness apart from Christ is impossible. We find dissatisfaction among the poor and rich alike, among the ignorant and the learned, among people and kings."

Looking for Yourself in God's Love Story

1. After reading though Ecclesiastes 1–3, would you describe this part of Ecclesiastes as an overly pessimistic missive? Why or why not?

2. Early Church Fathers regularly used the Latin phrase *Otium Sanctum*, which means "holy leisure." What activities and/or hobbies do you have that could be described as *holy leisure*? Do you think you have enough downtime in your schedule?

3. Stop and think about the last expensive but unnecessary purchase you made—perhaps a pair of beautiful leather boots or that cute new car you just *had* to have! How does buyer's remorse relate to the message of Ecclesiastes?

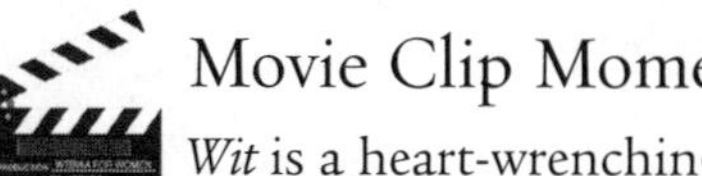

Movie Clip Moment

Wit is a heart-wrenching story. The screenplay (written by Mike Nichols and Emma Thompson) chronicles the journey of one woman—Professor Vivian Bearing, played by Emma Thompson—after she's been diagnosed with cancer. It's not an easy movie to sit through. It is profoundly sad, but it's definitely worth watching. Dr. Bearing's decline forces her to grapple with many of the same themes posed in Ecclesiastes, and the "living diary" style of the dialogue compels you to wrestle right along with her. One critic called Ms. Thompson's performance "mesmerizing," and I wholeheartedly agree. She convincingly portrays the inevitability and indignity of death, along with the subtle joy that comes with simply being alive one more day.

Pursued by a Prince

When I was growing up, I spent a few weeks every summer at a Christian camp called Lake Swan near Gainesville, Florida. We water-skied and played soccer and had great chapels and late night gabfests. And one of the most common topics of conversation was the Sadie Hawkins dance on the last night of camp. It wasn't actually a *dance*, though, because this was a pretty conservative Christian camp where the powers-that-be decided God's beloved couldn't boogie. We actually just stood around in our dress clothes in the cafeteria. But it was still the highlight—or the lowlight, depending on your perspective, personality and appearance—of the summer.

However, the real drama took place during the Sadie Hawkins Day race on the afternoon of the un-dance dance. The counselors would line up all the boys on one side of the soccer field and line up all the girls on the other side, facing the boys. Then, when the head counselor blew the whistle, each girl was supposed to chase whichever boy she wanted to go to the dance with that night. They'd probably get sued for having a Sadie Hawkins race today, because I'm sure some kids were emotionally damaged as a result! Especially the slow and the shy ones.

But the rest of us didn't know any better. So we spent countless hours before the race plotting who was going to chase whom. And for several years, the most wanted young man was Jeff McGarvey. Jeff was a preacher's kid from my hometown with curly brown hair and a killer jump shot. The guys admired his basketball skills, and most of the girls admired his legs in basketball shorts. He was the Brad Pitt of Lake Swan Camp.

One race day when I was 14 or 15, Jeff asked if he could talk to me outside the girls' cabins. This wasn't that unusual because we'd known each other since we were little—his mom was my piano teacher—and we were pretty good friends. I thought maybe he needed a ride home from camp. But that's not what he came to ask. He hemmed and hawed and then told me that he really wanted to go to the dance with me. When I said I'd like that, he told me where he'd run to when the whistle blew so that I could be the one to catch him.

The girls' line was buzzing when we lined up that day. And of course a lot of the chatter involved Jeff. But I didn't giggle or whisper about strategy with the rest of the girls, I just stood there grinning. And when the whistle sounded, I was the only girl who didn't take off running. I simply waited for a minute or two and then trotted over to the place where Jeff and I had agreed to meet.

That night I wore a peach polyester dress with spaghetti straps and Jeff wore a powder blue polyester leisure suit—I felt like we were the king and queen of camp! And I grinned so much my cheeks started to cramp! I kept thinking, *I can't believe Jeff McGarvey picked me.* There were girls who were much prettier. Girls who were much sweeter. Girls who'd come from much more impressive families. But Jeff McGarvey had picked me.

As sweet as that adolescent romance was, it pales next to the reality that the King of kings and Lord of lords has chosen us as His bride. The Creator of the Universe has a huge crush on us. The Prince of Peace pursues us. Abba adores us. He grins when He sees us coming. And despite our dirty and divided hearts, He has invited us to the dance of all dances!

What's the *Story* of This Particular Book?

The central characters in this historical romance are Solomon (David's smart son) and a woman from Shulam (also know as *Shulamith*). It's a wonderful love story with breathtaking imagery that promotes true friendship between husbands and wives, along with marital fidelity. However, at times the lyrics in this Old Testament poem read more like a Danielle Steele novel than Scripture! And sadly, because of the overtly sexual themes, this Song of all songs tends be shunned in Sunday School curriculums. Therefore, it's important to note that the overarching theme of this *Christological* (it's all about Jesus!) book is not about a *human* relationship—it's about the face-to-face intimacy we can have with God. He's not some faraway Supreme Being—He's the Lover of our souls.

Henrietta's Highlights on the Song of Songs

Her Synopsis
Jesus Christ, the Lover of Our Souls

Her Suggested Bible Readings
Day One: *Joyful Communion* (Song of Songs 1:1-7; 2:1-7)

Memorable Quotes from Dr. Mears
"The Song of Songs has been called the Christian's love song."

"The love of Solomon and the maid (Shulamith) illustrates the love between Jehovah and His people. This is seen in many passages in the Bible. Moreover, Solomon as a lover was a type of Christ (see Ephesians 5)."

Looking for Yourself in God's Love Story

1. Read Song of Songs 2:4-8. Describe your first brush with *true* love. How did you feel? Because of your affection, were you moved to do anything that now seems silly?

2. Read Song of Songs 4:1-5,9 and Psalm 139. Without qualification, what do you think your adoring Creator would say was your best feature?

3. Read Song of Songs 7:6-9. Shulamith's "hanging" breasts (remember in Song of Songs 4:5, Solomon described them as baby deer—in other words, "perky"—on their wedding day!) indicate that she's more mature now and probably breast-fed their children. Her body might not be as "hot" as it once was, but it can nourish others and sustain life. Who depends on you for *spiritual* nourishment?

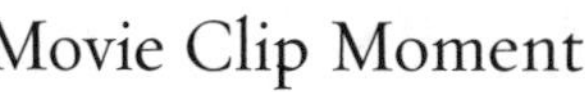

Movie Clip Moment

While I can't in good conscience recommend every scene in the 1999 romantic comedy *Notting Hill* (starring Hugh Grant and Julia Roberts), I can definitely recommend the last 10 minutes of this film to *adults*. The clip at the tail end of this Hollywood box-office smash is a sigh-inducing ode to true love (I must admit the end won't be nearly as heartwarming if you don't know the whole story). You could almost call this movie a modern adaptation of the Song of Songs, albeit without the Daughters of Jerusalem holding the lovebirds accountable so that they would save sex for their wedding night! But even with its far too permissible view of physical intimacy, this film has an overall positive view regarding romantic love and intimacy.

He Wants to Hold Your Hand

About 15 years ago I called my mom while gulping back sobs and told her I felt like my life was falling apart. I was in the middle of a difficult job change, a good friend had been killed in a car accident, and I'd just found out that another friend was having an affair. I was disillusioned and depressed and said I could no longer see the proverbial light at the end of the tunnel.

Mom listened to me for a long time and then told me that I should start reading the book of Isaiah. She said he had a lot to say about dark, desperate places. I must admit I wasn't initially enthused or encouraged by her advice. I didn't want her to tell me to study some ancient prophet—I wanted her to FedEx a plane ticket to a tropical island! Or at least tickets to a good movie and some chocolate!

But when I finally shut down my pity party and perused Isaiah, I discovered that mushrooms aren't the only things that grow in the dark. So does faith.

> I will lead the blind by ways they have not known, along unfamiliar paths I will guide them; I will turn the darkness into light before them and make the rough places smooth. These are the things I will do; I will not forsake them (Isaiah 42:16).

> Who among you fears the LORD and obeys the word of his servant? Let him who walks in the dark, who has no light, trust in the name of the LORD and rely on his God. But now, all you who light fires and provide yourselves with flaming torches, go, walk in the light of your fires and of the torches you have set ablaze. This is what you shall receive from my hand: You will lie down in torment (Isaiah 50:10-11).

Isaiah's metaphors are profoundly simple. When we find ourselves in gloomy circumstances and have to squint just to make out where to take our next step, we need to trust in God as our guide. We have to place our sweaty palms into His mighty right hand and give our spiritual pupils time to dilate. If we rely on our own ability to make the shadows disappear, we're going to be very sorry.

Reading this Old Testament prophecy didn't make the clouds in my life immediately vanish. It didn't magically shrink the hurdles in my way. It simply reminded me to pause and pray, to be still and listen for divine directions, and to quit whining and let God lead me.

What's the *Story* of This Particular Book?

Isaiah's story ushers in a section of the Old Testament commonly called the "major prophets" (Isaiah, Jeremiah, Lamentations, Ezekiel and Daniel). And "major" is certainly an apt description of Isaiah's tenure as God's mouthpiece! His ministry took place in Jerusalem while the kingdom was divided (739 to 686 B.C.) and spanned the reigns of four different rulers. His words are eloquent and inspirational, pointing to the imminent birth of the Messiah, Immanuel (see Isaiah 9:6-7). His message is also complex–it bounces back and forth between the temporal kingdom God established in Israel and the future realm of glory we'll experience in heaven.

Henrietta's Highlights on Isaiah

Her Synopsis
Isaiah Portrays Jesus Christ, the Messiah

Her Suggested Bible Readings
Sunday: *God's Case Against Judah* (Isaiah 1:1-18)
Monday: *Isaiah's Commission* (Isaiah 6)
Tuesday: *Christ–Israel's Hope* (Isaiah 7:10-16; 9)
Wednesday: *The Coming Kingdom* (Isaiah 11)
Thursday: *A Great God* (Isaiah 40)
Friday: *Christ Our Substitute* (Isaiah 53)
Saturday: *A Glorious Salvation* (Isaiah 55)

Memorable Quotes from Dr. Mears

"The prophet's chief duty was to deal with the moral and religious life of his own people during his day. The prophet was never sent while the nation was walking in obedience to God."

"God puts a telescope before the eyes of the prophets and lets them look far into the future. Especially do we find this spirit of expectation in Isaiah. We hear the prophet cry, 'He is coming!'"

Looking for Yourself in God's Love Story

1. Read Isaiah 6:6-10. Isaiah is the only prophet to be commissioned with a live coal—talk about a "heated" conversation! Describe a moment when you felt like your tongue was just burning up with something to say about God.

2. Read Isaiah 53, Matthew 27:1-55, Mark 15:1-41, Luke 23:1-49 and John 19:1-37. What common denominators do you find between Isaiah's prophecy about a suffering Savior and the eyewitness accounts of the crucifixion?

Movie Clip Moment

In chapter 23 of the lengthy but well-worth watching DVD *The Return of the King* (part three of *The Lord of the Rings* trilogy), there's a great clip in which a gruff and apprehensive dwarf named Gimli follows hunky Aragorn (played by Viggo Mortensen) into the Paths of the Dead—the ultimate dark and scary hike filled with dangerous stalagmites, an army of ghosts and an evil leader of the see-through guys. While it's obvious the little guy would have stumbled into big trouble if he'd ventured in there by himself, it's also obvious that he's going to be safe as long as he sticks close to his leader!

I Can't Get No Satisfaction

I had the privilege—and slight discomfort—of speaking at a church on Mother's Day. It was a privilege because any time I get to open my mouth and talk about Jesus is a delight. But it was a little awkward because I'm over 40 and single and Mother's Day is one of those celebrations earmarked for minivan-driving females with a gaggle of children, not chicks like me. Women whose doting husbands woke up early and cooked them a lovely breakfast, not women who woke up alone at the Fairfield Inn wondering if there'd be yogurt at the "continental" (a colorful euphemism for *sparse*) breakfast buffet. Women whose adorable children made them clay handprints with an "I Love You, Mom!" engraved during Sunday School class, not women whose only dependents are Jack Russell terriers! To say I felt a bit out of place in church that Sunday is an understatement. I felt like a platypus in a roomful of Persian cats.

Being single isn't unusual in our post-postmodern culture; as a matter of fact, the latest population statistics reveal there are more single people than those who've walked an aisle (and stayed married). However, being single *and* working in a Christ-centered women's ministry tends to be regarded as atypical. Perhaps because many of the women who attend Bible studies or retreats are married, the assumption is that those who lead the Bible studies or speak at the retreats will also be married. And since I'm an almost-over-the-hill anomaly, I'm often asked the question as to why I'm not married.

My favorite answer is that my future husband is lost and won't stop to ask for directions—which usually prompts giggles and helps steer the attention away from my lackluster private life and back toward Jesus. But frankly, most of the women I meet—whether married, single, divorced or widowed—struggle with similar issues: things like stress, guilt, disappointment and insecurity. Some of the married women I've met struggle with a loneliness that seems far more desperate than that experienced by the singles I know. The bottom line is that women from Vancouver to

Vermont long to be loved well, yet most are at least vaguely disappointed.

It's also been my experience that no matter which side of the marital fence we're standing on—the *till death do us part* side or the *maybe I'll try online dating* side—the grass typically looks greener in the other field. Many single women think that most of their problems could be solved by a good man, and many married women think most of their problems are caused by the he-doesn't-look-so-hot-now man that they married!

In either case, the men in our lives—present or unaccounted for—are given too much responsibility. No human shoulders are broad enough to bear all our burdens. Contrary to the plots of ripped-bodice romance novels, no man (or pirate!) will ever meet all our expectations. They can't, because they're sinners just like us. Even the godliest of human husbands can't love us *perfectly*. If you're waiting for a man to fulfill all your hopes and dreams, you're going to end up looking like the poster child for that well-known Rolling Stone's lyric, "I can't get no satisfaction." God is the only One who offers the unconditional love we're so desperate for—His is the only love that can truly satisfy us!

The theme of *searching for satisfaction in all the wrong places* is at the core of Jeremiah's message, too. He laments that God's people have wandered from Jehovah—their first love—and are foolishly jamming substitutes into the hole in their hearts that only He can fill. So Jeremiah the Prophet (not the bullfrog!) preaches and pleads for us to return to the One who adores us.

What's the *Story* of This Particular Book?

Jeremiah's book is like the songs sung in Memphis—it's basically the Old Testament version of the *blues*! The Israelites have spiraled out of control and God uses this red-eyed prophet (Jeremiah is commonly called the Weeping Prophet) as a mouthpiece for His disapproval. At one point in the story, God even instructs Jeremiah to wear a heavy wooden yoke around his neck to symbolize the slavery and oppression Israel will soon face in Babylon. But this true tale also includes four wonderful chapters (see chapters 30 to 33) of *comfort*, forecasting the loving restoration God has planned for His rebellious people.

Henrietta's Highlights on Jeremiah

Her Synopsis

Jeremiah Portrays Jesus Christ, the Righteous Branch

Her Suggested Bible Readings

Sunday: *Jeremiah Warns Judah* (Jeremiah 1:1-10; 2:1-13; 3:12,22-23; 4:14-19; 6)
Monday: *A Rebuke* (Jeremiah 7:1-15; 9:1-16; 17:5-18)
Tuesday: *The Potter* (Jeremiah 18:1-17)
Wednesday: *The Faithless Shepherds* (Jeremiah 23)
Thursday: *Repentance and Restoration* (Jeremiah 24–25)
Friday: *Israel's Last Days* (Jeremiah 30:18-24; 31)
Saturday: *The Overthrow of Judah* (Jeremiah 52)

Memorable Quotes from Dr. Mears

"God often chooses unlikely instruments to do His work."

"God has a plan for the life of every person. Some see clearly how their lives are to be used. Many learn to wait upon God and trust Him for the outcome. These latter cannot understand the ways of the Lord, but they believe His promises. Jeremiah must have been one of these."

"Hudson Taylor one time wrote, 'God delights to trust a trustworthy child with a trial.' How God must have trusted Jeremiah!"

Looking for Yourself in God's Love Story

1. Jesus quoted Jeremiah when He cleansed the Temple from a gang of self-centered capitalists (see Matthew 21:12-13; Jeremiah 7:11). What other similarities can you find between the Prince of Peace and this broken-hearted, Old Testament prophet? Jeremiah 11:21, 12:6, 16:2 and 31:31-37 provide some helpful hints!

2. Read Jeremiah 18:1-12. In "regular" words, how would you explain the main point of this analogy?

3. There are several other places in the Bible in which the relationship between a potter and clay is used to illustrate the relationship between God and humanity (see Isaiah 45:9; 64:8; Romans 9:21; 2 Corinthians 4:7). What adjectives come to mind when you ponder the connection between our heavenly Father and His personal "play dough"?

Movie Clip Moment

Hotel Rwanda is a powerful film, based on the horrific genocide that took place in the African country of Rwanda in the mid-1990s. Actor Don Cheadle plays a Hutu hotel manager named Paul Rusesabagina, who risked his life by opening his hotel rooms—and heart—to both Tutsi and Hutu refugees during the darkest days of violence. (The civil war was between these two African tribes: Hutu militants killed approximately 1 million Tutsis in just a little over 3 months.) This movie portrays a country spiraling out of control—not unlike ancient Israel—and Don Cheadle portrays a man who stood up for what was right in the midst of unspeakable evil—not unlike Jeremiah. (The real Paul Rusesabagina was recognized for his heroism when he received the Immortal Chaplains Prize for Humanity in 2000.)

A Lot of Grief Observed

When my younger brother, John, was just a little guy, he was captivated by all kinds of creatures. Quite a few of his animal "companions" were snuck into the house without our parent's knowledge, much less consent. Once Mom discovered hundreds of tadpoles floating in pie pans under his bed after the first few frogs migrated out into the carpeting! John also had several parent-approved pets, like two dogs, an aquarium full of fish and a turtle named Myrtle.

I like animals a lot too, although I prefer warm-blooded ones like puppies and horses. I never really acquired John's affection for amphibians, probably because they don't typically come when you call them or perform tricks for treats. Moreover, turtles tend to be a bit pokey in my opinion. But John adored Myrtle. He even smuggled him/her (I'm not sure how to determine turtle gender) into bed with him every night. I'm pretty sure Mom knew he was sleeping with his small green friend, but I guess after the tadpole fiasco she was thankful it was such a mild transgression of house rules.

Unfortunately, his nightly misdemeanors with Myrtle ended tragically. I remember him racing into the kitchen in tears one morning crying that Myrtle had died. Mom—knowing that John had likely killed the turtle by rolling over on it during the night—tried to console him by saying that Myrtle must've died peacefully in her sleep because it was just her time to go. And I'll never forget the way he looked up, his adorable face streaked with tears, and said, "No, Mama . . . I killed Myrtle." His little-boy sorrow was every bit as real as the grown-up grief I've experienced.

What's the *Story* of This Particular Book?

It's commonly agreed that Jeremiah, the Weeping Prophet, wrote this very sad book documenting Jerusalem's destruction at the hands of the Babylonian king Nebuchadnezzar and his army of bullies. The five "laments"—or *loud cries*—in Lamentations communicate the Israelites' sadness over the betrayal of their political allies, their indignation at God's disciplinary wrath, Jeremiah's personal grief, their desire to see their enemies punished, and a desperate plea for restoration. These Old Testament lyrics tell a tale of sorrow, regret and consequence.

Henrietta's Highlights on Lamentations

Her Synopsis
Lamentations Portrays Jesus Christ, the Righteous Branch

Her Suggested Bible Readings
Day One: *Comfort to the Sorrowing* (Lamentations 1–5)

Memorable Quote from Dr. Mears
"Above the clouds of the poet's weeping over the sins of his people, God's sun is shining."

Looking for Yourself in God's Love Story

Read Lamentations 3:22-25. Describe the gracious promise of God—given in the midst of His people's mourning—in your own words.

Movie Clip Moment

Robert Redford directed a movie titled *Ordinary People* (1980), and it is filled with lament. The storyline follows the emotional decline of a wealthy family in the throes of grief after the death of the oldest son in an accident, which the youngest son survived. Mary Tyler Moore plays the embittered mother, Beth—a woman who's not very likable at first, but who provides a striking portrait of how unexpressed sorrow can poison one's soul.

Flinging Luggage and Frosty Hearts

I considered using my luggage as a weapon recently. Not to inflict mass destruction, mind you, but to get an obnoxious man on the airport shuttle to shut up! He was one of those look-I'm-important-because-I'm-on-my-cell-phone types, who didn't consider how his midnight bellowing was impacting the rest of us who had the misfortune to be wedged into the van with him. The man sitting beside him even had his fingers jammed pointedly in his ears. But his posture was to no avail because Mr. Loud Talker kept jabbering. *That's* when I pondered whacking him really hard with my roll-aboard!

You've probably been in a similar situation when you've had to deal with someone who got on your very last nerve—maybe some shrill woman in a theme sweater who constantly whines in small group. Perhaps you've pondered bonking her ever so gently with a potted plant! Frankly, I think Christians who *don't* contemplate whacking perpetual whiners from time to time are either saints or faking it, because getting irritated by other believers is a normal occurrence in the Body of Christ. It's when you *don't ever* struggle with unsuitable emotion that you might need to worry.

Let me explain.

Recently I had dinner with a good friend and her family. She and her husband were unfailingly polite: They didn't raise their voices when their kids spilled food; they chatted about current events; and they cleaned up like clockwork. But when I had some time alone with my friend and asked a few hard questions, the walls of "appropriate" behavior came crashing down and she wept over the lack of emotion in her marriage. She said that she and her husband were basically just coexisting as roommates—that the "peace" in their home was really whitewashed apathy. She longed to rekindle the honest emotion that used to define them and have a *real* relationship—warts and all—once more.

What about you? Do you feel like you're just going through the motions of ministry? Has the low-grade fever of apathy begun to weaken your compassion for others? Does your soul seem numb?

If so, it's time to emulate Ezekiel and schedule some divine surgery:

> And I will give you a new heart and put a new spirit in you; I will remove from you your heart of stone and give you a heart of flesh (Ezekiel 36:26).

Don't neglect the post-op recuperation after God operates either. Maybe you could take a few vacation days away from people who rub you the wrong way. Or at least take a long walk in the park. Watch a movie that makes you laugh so hard you cry. Indulge in a few pieces of dark chocolate. Ask the Holy Spirit to help you cultivate a healthier, tender heart so as to love God and His people better. But whatever you do, please resist the urge to assault someone with a Samsonite!

What's the *Story* of This Particular Book?

The prophet Ezekiel was booted to Babylon when the second wave of Israelites was forced out of Jerusalem in 597 B.C. His confinement compels him to leap on stage and belt out a warning to the rest of God's people still residing in the Holy City. His unsolicited advice is essentially this: "Y'all better shape up or God's going to ship you out, and you're going to end up behind bars in Babylon like the rest of us!" But midway through his monologue, Ezekiel shifts gears and segues from a dire admonition into an inspirational vision about the amazing plans God has for Israel's future—the proverbial bright morning after their dark season of discipline.

Henrietta's Highlights on Ezekiel

Her Synopsis
Ezekiel Portrays Jesus Christ, the Son of Man

Her Suggested Bible Readings
Sunday: *The Prophet's Call* (Ezekiel 2:1–3:9)
Monday: *The Prophet a Watchman* (Ezekiel 3:10-27)
Tuesday: *Israel Shall Be Saved* (Ezekiel 11:14-21; 28:25-26)
Wednesday: *Israel's Sins* (Ezekiel 22:3-31)
Thursday: *Israel's Future* (Ezekiel 34)
Friday: *Israel's Restoration* (Ezekiel 36)
Saturday: *Vision of the Dry Bones* (Ezekiel 37:1-14)

Memorable Quotes from Dr. Mears
"God needed a voice to warn the people and to remind them of the reason all these calamities had befallen them."

"God's greatest communications can only be made by his servants whose own hearts have been broken. The instrument in God's hands must personally be ready to share in suffering with others. Jesus' body was broken for us."

"God's judgment on sin is certain and severe. His redemption is equally certain when it is welcomed by the human heart."

"God will gather together His scattered people. God says over and over, 'I will, I will.'"

Looking for Yourself in God's Love Story

1. The name "Ezekiel" means "God strengthens"—what are some ways in which God has strengthened you recently?

2. Rainbows are listed several times in Scripture—read Genesis 9:11-17, Ezekiel 1:28, Revelation 4:3 and 10:1.

Noah saw one after a storm, Ezekiel saw it during the storm, and John saw one when the storm was over—but all the rainbows reflected God's mercy. What do you think/feel when you see a rainbow?

3. Toward the end of Ezekiel, there's an incredible scene in which God breathes new life into dry bones (see 37:1-14). He doesn't simply perk-up folks who are feeling puny—He resurrects completely desiccated skeletons! What long-dead dreams do you need God to revive in your heart?

Movie Clip Moment

One of the best chick flicks of all times is *Steel Magnolias,* a tale about family, friendship and love that's willing to leap over the far side of the moon! There's a touching scene near the end of the story that prompts even manly men to reach for the Kleenex. Sally Field plays a totally together Southern belle who falls apart after her daughter's funeral. The first time I witnessed her raw grief in the theater, I cried like a baby. And it still never fails to cause waterworks when I watch it now—even though I know how it ends! If you're feeling numb, if perhaps your heart *feels* like a valley of dusty bones, this film might be the onion your arid eyes need.

DANIEL

Dangerous Games and a Very Protective Dad

After my parents divorced, I spent most weekends at my dad's ranch out in the country. He had horses and cows and dirt bikes—for an all-American tomboy like me, it was paradise! One of my favorite pastimes on the farm was a game called Psych the Cows. I'd talk my less rambunctious stepbrother, Ricky, into perching in a tree near the cow pasture, then I'd waltz out toward the herd of Holsteins and shake a coffee can full of feed. Because that was how Dad called them to the barn—it was a very effective bovine dinner bell—they'd all look up from grazing and begin to gallop after me.

The exhilarating part of this game was when the cows really got going and closed in directly behind me on the narrow trail. I'd sprint as fast as I could—usually squealing with glee—and hope to make it to the low-hanging branch where Ricky sat wide-eyed before the stampede trampled me into a grease spot! The only downside to Psych the Cows was that they were only susceptible to trickery a few times each weekend. Once they realized the ruse, they calmly returned to chewing cud and ignored me no matter how vigorously I rattled the can.

One Saturday, after the cows stopped taking part in our tomfoolery, I turned to a weary Ricky and said, "Hey, let's go try to trick the bull!" He immediately objected and reminded me that Dad said we weren't allowed anywhere near the dangerous Texas Longhorn he'd recently bought to befriend our lady cows. Unfortunately, the planned romance went bust when it became apparent that the bull was too aggressive to breed. The big guy was ostracized to a pasture all alone until Dad could figure out what to do with him.

I assured Ricky that we wouldn't even get close to the bull because we'd practice our silent Indian walk and sneak through the woods to the *opposite* side of the field from where the bull *always* grazed. I promised him that we'd have a huge head start and that it'd be the most exiting game we'd ever played! Ricky wasn't convinced, but he reluctantly followed far behind me as we heel-toed through the pine needles toward our archenemy.

Unfortunately, after carefully making our way to the strategic "safe" zone, we looked up to find that the bull wasn't in his usual place. Instead of being about 100 yards away, he was standing directly in front of us with his massive head lowered and nostrils flaring. If bulls could talk, he was saying something along the lines of, "I'm about to poke my horns right into your hiney, little girl!" I can still remember the white-hot fear that coursed through me. I screamed and dropped the coffee can and took off running with the Texas killing machine right on my heels.

Somehow I managed to stay ahead of him, but as the fence loomed closer, I realized that I didn't have enough time to stop and crawl through the barbed wire. So I streaked toward the closest post, thinking I could jump on the strands of wire and vault over out of harm's way. When I hopped on the top strand, however, the *U*-shaped nail holding it in place popped loose and I slid down the wire until one of the barbs pierced my backside, skewering me in place. Fortunately Dad heard my shrieks and ran up the hill to rescue me! He hit the bull in the head, hoisted me off the barbed wire, and carried me up to the house to bandage my cuts and bruises.

I can't help but grin when I look back at those adolescent misadventures—and breathe a big sigh of gratitude for having a dad who could double as a bodyguard!

What's the *Story* of This Particular Book?

The true story of Daniel—an interpreter of dreams who was full of integrity—and his trio of young buddies with weird names (Shadrach, Meshach and Abednego) took place while the Israelites were suffering in captivity in Babylon. They no doubt needed reminding that their heavenly Father was powerful and able to deliver them from the scary situation in which they found themselves. Hearing about how God shielded Daniel and his friends from harm in a blazing furnace surely encouraged His people, and the way God protected Daniel in a lion's den (see Daniel 6) makes Him the most heroic "Dad" in all of history! This prophetic book also includes colorful apocalyptic visions regarding the end of the earth as we know it.

Henrietta's Highlights on Daniel

Her Synopsis
Daniel Portrays Jesus Christ, the Smiting Stone

Her Suggested Bible Readings
Sunday: *Daniel the Captive* (Daniel 1–2)
Monday: *Nebuchadnezzar, the Proud King* (Daniel 3–4)
Tuesday: *Belshazzar's Reign* (Daniel 5:7-8)
Wednesday: *Darius's Reign* (Daniel 6–9)
Thursday: *God's Glory* (Daniel 10)
Friday: *The Conflict of Kings* (Daniel 11)
Saturday: *Daniel's Last Message* (Daniel 12)

Memorable Quotes from Dr. Mears
"Daniel has been called the prophet of dreams. God revealed to him His secrets."

"Daniel was, like Joseph, God's candle shining in pagan darkness."

"Daniel was thrown into the den of lions, but he fell into the hands of the living God. The world cannot breed a lion that God cannot tame."

Looking for Yourself in God's Love Story

1. Compare the scene in Daniel 3:8-18 with Peter's New Testament admonition about Christians submitting to government authorities in 1 Peter 2:13-17. When do you think it's okay in God's eyes for us to defy the regulations established by human rulers?

2. Daniel refers to God as the "Ancient of Days" (Daniel 7:9,13,22), illustrating His absolute authority over

human history. What name would you give God to illustrate His protective role in your personal history?

Movie Clip Moment

The sci-fi movie *Signs*, starring Mel Gibson, paints a creative picture of supernatural protection. While it's not necessarily a Christ-centered film (though there is a recurrent theme about the importance of faith), there's still a great message about being delivered by something/someone bigger than us. The illustration-friendly clip takes place at the end of the drama, when the evil alien is just about to bonk the good human being, but instead gets walloped by a baseball bat. Just rent the movie—it'll make sense then!

Against All Odds

I tickle myself at the measures I'm willing to go through in order to attract the opposite sex. In my svelte twenties I would never have dreamed that one day I'd wear torture devices disguised as undergarments. They're called "body shapers," but a more suitable label would be "breath killers" because it's difficult to inhale and exhale when you've got python panties strangling you from ribcage to waist!

Though I know the size of my stomach isn't as important as the size of my heart, I'll still gladly sacrifice lung capacity for a shot at true love. Most of my friends would, too! At some silly emotional level, we all long for the kind of romance we've seen in the movies. We've nurtured daydreams about having a relationship like that of Humphrey Bogart and Lauren Bacall, Spencer Tracy and Katherine Hepburn, or—more recently—Richard Gere and Julia Roberts.

You remember the movie *Pretty Woman*, don't you? Julia Roberts plays Vivian, a gorgeous, warm-hearted prostitute, while Richard Gere plays Edward, a successful but emotionally aloof businessman. After hiring her to masquerade as his date at a few important business functions (and spending scads of money on her makeover), Edward falls madly in love with Vivian, despite the fact that she sells her body for money. Their fictitious courtship was so compelling that it became one of the highest-grossing romantic comedies in Hollywood history.

If you really think about it, however, their romance is unrealistic. I mean, why in the world would a wealthy, handsome and well-educated entrepreneur settle on a streetwalker? The plotline just doesn't make sense. But interestingly enough, it parallels a real relationship nestled in the pages of the Old Testament, a beautiful love story about a girl named Gomer and a guy named Hosea.

What's the *Story* of This Particular Book?

Hosea is the first book in a 12-book section called the Minor Prophets. I used to think they were labeled "minor" because they were penned by petite authors, but they're actually called that because of their relatively short lengths! This particular prophecy is probably the most well loved of the dozen because of the way Gomer and Hosea's story is tucked inside the larger story of Jehovah's commitment to Israel. Hosea's devotion to his adulterous wife is a striking human portrait of our heavenly Husband's steadfast loyalty to us.

Henrietta's Highlights on Hosea

Her Synopsis
Jesus Christ, Healer of the Backslider

Her Suggested Bible Readings
Day One: *Israel's Willful Ignorance* (Hosea 4)
Day Two: *Israel's Glorious Future* (Hosea 3; 14)

Memorable Quotes from Dr. Mears
"The hero of this book, Hosea, is one of the greatest lovers in all literature. We find his love so strong that even the worst actions of an unfaithful wife could not kill it."

"God has agonized over His rebellious people and will not give them up. His mercy is kindled and He says, 'I will heal their waywardness and love them freely' (Hosea 14:4)."

Looking for Yourself in God's Love Story

1. Read Hosea 1–3. Many people—including theologian and church father John Calvin—have questioned why God would ask one of His children to marry a woman He knew would commit adultery. If you had to write a paper or engage in debate on this subject, how would you *justify* God's asking Hosea to marry a "whore"?

2. Reread Hosea 2:6 in the *New American Standard* version of the Bible (if you don't have this version, you can look

it up online at www.biblegateway.com). Can you think of a time when God built a "hedge" to keep you from making a bad decision and ultimately hurting yourself?

3. Read Exodus 4:22-23 and Isaiah 54:5. Hosea uses both God-as-our-Father and God-as-our-Husband to illustrate our relationship with Him. Which one makes you feel more secure?

Movie Clip Moment

Of course, it's got to be *Pretty Woman*! However, I do recommend watching the "Clean Flicks" version, if you can find one, so as to screen out the racy parts.

Ugly Conduct, Unmerited Compassion

After a childhood of relative compliance, I jumped into the fray of teenaged rebellion with gusto. Within weeks of making some new wild girlfriends in high school, I left my morals in the dust and became a passionate partier. We pilfered bottles of liquor from the more permissive parents' liquor cabinets (our house was a "dry" province) and found some cute boys who agreed to sell us marijuana at a discount.

My friends' parents never suspected that we were prodigals. We were all from "good" families, were on the honor roll and were involved in wholesome extracurricular activities like athletics and student government. By my parents couldn't help but notice the change in me. I'd gone from being a gregarious, well-mannered daughter to a sullen, disrespectful young woman who didn't tell stories at dinner anymore.

My stepfather attributed my personality makeover to puberty, but my wise mom knew that my averted eyes and moodiness were clear outward signs of inner upheaval. She diagnosed me with a wandering heart problem and prescribed a few weeks at a Christian camp to heal it. To say I wasn't too happy about her course of action is an understatement—none of my popular friends were being shipped off for the summer to some cheesy place with musty cabins filled with a bunch of Goody Two-shoes! So I argued and poked out my bottom lip and begged Mom to change her mind, but she was immovable and told me to start packing.

Once I arrived at Lake Swan Camp, my resolve to hate it didn't last very long. The other campers weren't pasty nerds, the counselors were really cool and the water skiing was a blast! Plus, every night there was some engaging speaker talking about Jesus. One was a guy named Josh McDowell. He talked about how if

Jesus lived in us, He should stick out—how it should be apparent to anyone watching us that we were committed to Christ above all else. I don't remember exactly what else he said, but I felt like he was talking directly to me, and I couldn't get up the aisle fast enough. I tearfully confessed all the crud I'd been doing and prayed for God to forgive me and clean me up.

Afterward, I was so excited about His divine pardon that I couldn't sleep, but my insomnia was also due to anxiety about what I was going to tell mom. Just a few months earlier I'd gotten in big trouble for calling my little brother a "butthole," and I knew that drinking piña coladas and smoking pot were *way* worse than that. I worried that I might be facing hard time at a juvenile detention facility, or at least being grounded until I was 30. I fretted about the severity of my punishment for the rest of my camp stay and the long drive home.

The minute the car pulled into our driveway, Mom came running outside and hugged me hard—which of course caused me to dissolve into sobs and choke out the whole wretched tale of my hellion season. When I had finished, I winced and waited for her rebuke, a sharp intake of breath or a stern look of disapproval. But they never came. Instead she smiled, put her hands on my wet cheeks and pulled me into another embrace.

What's the *Story* of This Particular Book?

Joel uses the phrase "the day of the Lord" five times to forecast God's impending judgment. In other words, he tells Israel, "You're about to get in really big trouble," over and over again! However, in contrast to Joel's sober warning, this brief book ends on a redemptive note when Joel talks about the *absolute restoration*—material, spiritual and national—that God's people will ultimately enjoy (see Joel 2:18-32; 3). All of their wounds will be healed when their heavenly Father wraps them up into a giant restorative hug!

Henrietta's Highlights on Joel

Her Synopsis
Jesus Christ, Restorer

Her Suggested Bible Readings
Day One: *Punishment and Blessing* (Joel 2)
Day Two: *The Restoration of Israel* (Joel 3)

Memorable Quote from Dr. Mears
"Spiritual deliverance is the central promise of the book of Joel."

Looking for Yourself in God's Love Story

Some of God's most comforting words to His rebellious children are recorded in Joel: "I will repay you for the years the locusts have eaten" (Joel 2:25). Basically, our heavenly Father is embracing His prodigal children and saying, "In spite of everything you've done, I still love you. Shhhh, don't cry. Everything's going to be okay." What chapter in your life is best described by this reassuring promise from the Lord?

Movie Clip Moment

Antwone Fisher is another one of those inspirational films that's based on a true story. This one chronicles the life of Antwone Fisher (now an acclaimed screenwriter) who joined the Navy to escape a horrible foster-home life. But Fish's anger—fuelled by years of abuse—made him someone who didn't "play well with others." His violent behavior landed him in a naval psychiatrist's office (the psychiatrist is played by Denzel Washington) in a last-ditch effort to salvage his military career. There's a wonderful scene near the end of the movie between Denzel and Fisher that captures the heart of redemption. One more repentant prodigal welcomed home!

Boondoggled by Bracelets and Other Baubles

I'm over 40 and single, but the lack of a diamond on my left hand is certainly not due to a lack of effort. Frankly, I've been on more blind dates than I care to remember, and the older I get, the more rarely *good* dates happen. For this reason, I was delighted when I was set up with a great, godly guy that we'll call Hal.

The minute we met, I was taken in by his broad grin, even broader shoulders and deep voice. By the time the waiter came to clear our dinner plates, I was thoroughly charmed. Hal was authentic and witty. He wasn't unhealthily attached to his mother or overly fond of cats. He smelled nice and didn't wear a pinky ring. Plus, we had lots of stuff in common—both of us were competitive cyclists, we'd both recently been to Israel, and we'd both been scuba diving at the exact same site in Central America. And finally, his last name was "Wright," so I thought, "This really must be my dream man!"

At the end of our date, we walked outside to admire a gorgeous full moon. It was very picturesque and romantic and I found myself thinking, *It just couldn't get much better than this!* We talked a little longer and made plans to get together the next day, and then Hal moved forward to hug me. As he was leaning down, I reached up—attempting to be demure—to place my hand on his shoulder. But when I did, the clasp on my bracelet got caught in the loose weave of my sweater and trapped my hand to my breast.

I flailed, desperately trying to free myself, before Hal made contact. However the more I wiggled, the more tangled I got. So when he wrapped his strong arms around me—in a perfectly appropriate, un-lusty way—I couldn't help but caress his chest with my bound appendage! He stepped back quickly, I think more than a little surprised by my "assertiveness," and said something polite like, "Thank you for a wonderful evening." I mumbled an embarrassed, "Thank you, too," in response, all the while twirling my snarled wrist in little circles.

When I turned away from his truck and walked toward the door, I got so tickled by my faux pas that I started giggling. Here I was, thinking that I'd finally achieved blind-date utopia, only to be boondoggled by a bracelet. The whole experience was an effective reminder that perfection is a big, fat fable! We are comically blemished people existing on a broken planet.

What's the *Story* of This Particular Book?

The Israelites in Amos's era had become deluded, too, thinking that they were living in utopia! During this season of biblical history, Judah (the Southern Kingdom) was busy celebrating her economic prosperity. God's people spent a lot of time at the mall—buying whatever their fickle hearts desired—and hanging out at spas, getting pedicures and being pampered. They were thinking, *It just doesn't get much better than this!* But their self-centered spending took their minds off God. So God chose Amos, a shepherd from Tekoa, to be His mouthpiece to shout a warning at His wandering sheep.

Henrietta's Highlights on Amos

Her Synopsis
Jesus Christ, Heavenly Husbandman

Her Suggested Bible Readings
Day One: *Personal Admonitions* (Amos 3:1-7; 4:6-12)
Day Two: *The Prophet's Intercession* (Amos 7–8)
Day Three: *Future Kingdom Blessings* (Amos 9)

Memorable Quotes from Dr. Mears
"Amos was not the only prophet of his day. God had sent a great galaxy of messengers to save His people from the destruction they were inevitably facing."

"Amos feared God so much that he feared no one else at all."

"God always warns before a punishment, yes, and offers a way of escape. God denounces sin, but He offers a remedy for sin."

Looking for Yourself in God's Love Story

1. Read Amos 4:1-5. "Cows of Bashan" refers to a specific breed of fancy cattle from Samaria. So when Amos uses that as a metaphor, he's indicting the wealthy Israelite women for behaving arrogantly, like they're better than everyone else. Do you know any Christians who act superior to other people? How does their haughty behavior affect you?

2. Amos is relentless in his call for social compassion. He strongly encourages the Israelites to be fair in their business dealings and to share their resources with those less fortunate (see Amos 5:11-15). What are some practical ways that we as Christians can care for the poor in our culture? What are you doing personally to love the "least" of these?

Movie Clip Moment

Legally Blonde is a pretty light movie about a pretty, spoiled chick named Elle Woods (played by Reese Witherspoon), who goes to Harvard Law School. Fortunately, Elle has a complete change of heart during the course of the story—maturing from selfish sorority girl to altruistic attorney. Her transformation is not unlike the one Amos encourages the people of Judah to make—from selfish and arrogant to compassionate and humble.

Beware of Bullies

I made a pet purchase last month that isn't turning out quite like I'd planned. I live out in the country, and probably as a result of reading too many James Herriot novels as a child (he wrote *All Creatures Great and Small*, and many other books filled with amusing stories about the animals he encountered as a country veterinarian), I nurse visions about all kinds of creatures living in peaceful accord on my wee acre-and-a-quarter. I bought a couple of Nigerian Dwarf goats to frolic with my Jack Russell terriers, Dottie and Harley.

I spent months researching these animals online because I wanted to make sure I was getting the smartest, most sociable and least stinky goats possible. That's why I settled on the Nigerian Dwarf breed—supposedly they're the pick-of-the-litter when it comes to four-legged animals capable of eating a tin can! I also chose *girl* goats because boys (*Billy* goats) have a reputation for being aggressive and odiferous.

After making my pick online, I named the pair Rosie and Madeleine (after Rosa Parks and Madeleine L'Engle—my favorite bus-riding activist and my favorite female author, respectively) and had a hilly section of my property fenced for their impending arrival. Then the breeder informed me that Maddie was pregnant, so I could only bring Rosie home for now—which, I reasoned, was probably a blessing in disguise, because it would allow the dogs to acclimatize to one new yard peer at a time.

Rosie was outfitted with a darling red collar for her homecoming (she's very cute "yard art," capable of slowing traffic) and was showered with treats to help make her transition from busy farm to quiet little hill easier. I waited a few days to formally introduce her to Dottie (Harley's a sissy, so I always let him go last) and held both of them on leashes while one sniffed and the other stared. Then I let them go—sure they would be fast friends for the rest of their furry little lives. Rosie backed cautiously toward her stall and Dottie trotted toward her with a happy bark as if to say, "Welcome to my yard!"

My dream of a harmonious commune of creatures was shattered when Rosie suddenly galloped forward, lowered her head and butted Dottie right on the noggin, sending her sprawling paws over tail and yelping in terror. After their collision, I realized that in lieu of a Billy goat, I'd come home with an innocent-looking *bully* goat!

What's the *Story* of This Particular Book?

Well, for starters, it's short—the shortest book in the entire Old Testament—and it's about bullies! To be more specific, this prophecy relates to the pagan nation of Edom, which delighted in shoving Israel around. The gist of Obadiah's message to these mean-spirited oppressors is that God is going to wipe them out as punishment for picking on His kids.

Henrietta's Highlights on Obadiah

Her Synopsis
Obadiah Portrays Jesus Christ, Our Savior

Her Suggested Bible Reading
Day One: *Doom and Deliverance* (Obadiah verses 1-21)

Memorable Quote from Dr. Mears
"God's judgment on Edom as Israel's notable enemy should warn nations today that God has not cast off His people and nations that oppress them will surely bring down His judgments (Genesis 12:3)."

Looking for Yourself in God's Love Story

1. Read Genesis 25–26. The Edomites were descendants of Esau and had inherited not only his penchant for wild living but also his disdain for his brother (the Edomites and Israelites were essentially first cousins). How does this bitterness among relatives illustrate rebellion against God? (Read Deuteronomy 23:7 for a hint.)

2. Read Matthew 2. How is God's warning in Obadiah partly fulfilled through the birth of Jesus, under the nose of King Herod (who was half-Edomite)?

Movie Clip Moment

In the dramatic military thriller *A Few Good Men* (1992), Jack Nicholson plays a mean Marine colonel by the name of Nathan Jessup. The plot involves the accidental murder of a young marine, Private Santiago, and the ensuing cover-up. Much of the action takes place in a courtroom where two of Santiago's colleagues are being tried for his murder. The Obadiah moment takes place near the end of the film, when attorney Lieutenant Daniel Kaffee (played by Tom Cruise) corners Nicholson on the stand, causing him (Nicholson) to blow his cool and bellow, "You can't handle the truth!" Hot-headed Nicholson is a very believable bully–I think he might be part Edomite! This fast-paced, adult-oriented drama also stars Demi Moore, Kevin Bacon and Kiefer Sutherland.

Stubbornness Isn't a Spiritual Gift

My friends will tell you that I'm a terrible patient and tenacious when it comes to physical pain. I come by my stoicism naturally because my mother—who's an otherwise cute, well-mannered, petite woman—has the pain threshold of a burly, ax-wielding, beer-chugging lumberjack. The subtle message in our home was that if you didn't have pneumonia or a compound fracture, you should just suck it up and quit being a baby!

I used to think my ability to endure pain without being a "sissy" was admirable, until a few years ago when I found out the hard way how dangerous and damaging it can be to grin and bear it. I'd hurt my back trail running on Pike's Peak and had ignored the throbbing for several days, thinking I could just gobble some ibuprofen and it'd go away (plus, my back always hurts because I was run over by a car when I was little).

However, after gritting my teeth through a business trip and several speaking engagements, I swallowed my pride and went to a doctor. He poked around a little—with what seemed to be distracted irritation—and asked me to rate my discomfort on a scale of 1 to 10. Since I didn't want to sound like a hypochondriac and reasoned that 10 must represent death, I gave it a 2 or 3. After which, he prescribed more ibuprofen and suggested I rent some good movies and "lay low" for the weekend.

I shuffled out of his office embarrassed and determined never to bother a busy, brilliant physician again. I also decided to disregard his advice about rest and cure my wimpy back with a long mountain bike ride. But a few months—and several biking, camping and ski trips—later, my back was worse than ever. I could barely walk, couldn't sleep and was hobbled by horrible burning, stabbing sensations up and down my legs.

Ultimately, after a belated MRI, that same doc diagnosed me with two completely ruptured discs. He apologized profusely, saying that he never would've suspected that I had such a severe injury because my complaints about pain were so minimal. I ended up having major surgery, which was relatively successful–though I can't run anymore, have a hard time bending over and had to give up my dreams of becoming a limbo champion!

I was foolish to think of weakness as inexcusable instead of inevitable. Admitting we hurt and asking for help is wholly appropriate. Spiritually speaking, we actually have to *acknowledge our sickness in order to be made well*!

What's the *Story* of This Particular Book?

Jonah, the minor prophet most famous for hitching a ride in the belly of a whale, was also an obstinate man who had a hard time admitting weakness. After finally obeying God's directive to preach to the pagans in Nineveh (the whale ride was a divine incentive), he gets to play a part in a huge national revival (see Jonah 3). But instead of celebrating God's grace for the Assyrian stinkers, Jonah stalks off in a big huff. Even when God points out his bad attitude, he stubbornly refuses to admit any fault (see Jonah 4). Funny how he could recognize everybody else's spiritual sickness, but chose to ignore his own!

Henrietta's Highlights on Jonah

Her Synopsis
Jesus Christ, Our Resurrection and Life

Her Suggested Bible Readings
Day One: *A Fish Story* (Jonah 1-2)
Day Two: *An Obedient Prophet* (Jonah 3-4)

Memorable Quotes from Dr. Mears
"Jonah is the test book of the Bible. It challenges our faith."

"No doubt, two things hindered Jonah when God told him to go to Nineveh–his pride of self and his scorn of the rest of the world."

Looking for Yourself in God's Love Story

1. Read Matthew 12:40. What else do you think Jonah and our Savior, Jesus, have in common?

2. Compare Jonah's "repentance prayer" in chapter 2 with his refusal to be glad about God's mercy for Nineveh in chapter 4. When have you swung from sincere penitence to stubborn pride in a short period of time?

Movie Clip Moment

Pixar's animated 2006 release *Cars* tells the story of a stubborn little racecar who was made in the mold of Jonah. Lightning McQueen is a prideful coupe who doesn't care for other cars and doesn't think he needs any help—that is, until he accidentally veers onto Route 66 and learns some very important life lessons. This flick's rated G (though it has a few mild tongue-in-cheek sexual innuendos) and has been given the family green light by several Christian publications and online movie websites.

Clinging to Crumbling Safeguards

Several years ago I went on a camping and climbing trip with members of a Christian organization in Northern California. I was really excited about the trip because I love the outdoors and was looking forward to rock climbing for the first time—but the trip turned out to be a bit more than I bargained for!

After huffing and puffing up a mountain trail for miles, lugging heavy backpacks, we finally made it to our campsite. Then, after eating what looked and tasted like potpourri, we crawled into our musty sleeping bags to get some rest before the real adventure began. Promptly at dawn, our wilderness instructors woke us up, fed us more "potpourri" and then started teaching us the technical skills we'd need to scale the sheer granite face that loomed a few hundred yards away. (I think I could've retained more of their lesson if they'd given me a Starbuck's mocha to go with the morning gruel!)

Still, by the time the detailed lecture was over, I was raring to go! I hurriedly strapped on my harness—hoping it didn't make my bottom look too big—because I was so anxious to attack the wall. Then, because the "beginner" route was taken, I walked over to the "advanced" area, reasoning that I'm pretty athletic and I'd be able to handle it.

I did for about a hundred feet. As a matter of fact, I shimmied up that rock so well that a small crowd of admirers gathered below. They were shouting cheers of encouragement like, "Way to go, Lisa! You're doing great!" and I found myself grinning with pride—until I got to a ledge that arched out over my head.

I couldn't figure out how to get around the precipice—the only option seemed to climb over it—which would leave me practically inverted, way, *way* above the ground. I wish I could tell you that I calmly assessed the situation and rose above the challenge. But I didn't. I panicked. I clung to my amateur handholds and begged God to save me. I told Him that I'd gladly go to Africa and live in a hovel and be a missionary for the rest of my life if He'd just *get me down*!

My friends below sensed my fear and called a couple of the instructors over to help me. They yelled for me to let go and trust the rope—assuring me that it would hold my weight—which sounded about as rational as telling someone, "Just jump out of the plane and we'll toss your parachute out after you!" Somewhere, deep in the recesses on my terrified brain, I knew they were telling me the truth, but I couldn't think logically—I was too concerned about becoming a human pancake!

It wasn't until muscle spasms weakened my grip that I finally trusted the rope like they told me to. When I was finally lowered to *terra firma* and looked up, I realized how silly I'd been to hang on to a pebble when there was a perfectly reliable system set up solely for my protection!

What's the *Story* of This Particular Book?

Micah's peers in Judah (the Southern Kingdom) were clinging to the wrong things, too. They foolishly thought they'd be saved from certain destruction by religiosity and ritual. They thought merely *looking* devout would keep them safe and secure from divine judgment. But God speaks through Micah—using a courtroom metaphor—to reveal how puny their spiritual "protection" really is. Of course, their vulnerability became really clear when their relatives in the Northern Kingdom were carted off to captivity in Babylon (God's version of a disciplinary time-out) just a few short years after Micah wrote this warning.

Henrietta's Highlights on Micah

Her Synopsis
Jesus Christ, Witness Against Rebellious Nations

Her Suggested Bible Readings
Day One: *A Message to the People* (Micah 1–2)
Day Two: *A Message to the Rulers* (Micah 3–4)
Day Three: *The Birth and Rejection of the King* (Micah 5)
Day Four: *A Message to the Chosen People* (Micah 6–7)

Memorable Quotes from Dr. Mears

"God is not asleep. He knows the sad condition of His people."

"Men and women are always trying to get back into the good graces of God with some outward religious service or some worldly rather than spiritual things. But remember 'the sacrifices of God are a broken spirit; a broken and contrite heart, O God, you will not despise' (Psalm 51:17)."

Looking for Yourself in God's Love Story

1. Read Micah 5:2-5 and Matthew 2:1-6. What's your favorite memory that includes this Christmas story?

2. Read "God's little instruction book" in Micah 6:8. How would you explain this divine directive in your own words?

Movie Clip Moment

I feel the need to qualify this action movie before even telling you the title because it's pretty silly—but it does have one great celluloid moment that illustrates the futility of human protective devices! The flick is called *Cliffhanger*, and it stars Sylvester Stallone, so you can probably imagine the heroic plotline. However, you don't have to watch the entire thing because the "drop" scene takes place at the very beginning (though the film as a whole is worthwhile to watch, as John Lithgow makes a very believable bad guy)!

Look Before You Leap

When my grandmother was a little girl, she had visions of Peter Pan-like grandeur. It wasn't that she was enamored with green tights or British kids in pajamas, but she desperately wanted to fly. I guess most kids are captivated with thoughts about spreading their arms and riding on the wings of the wind—at one time or another, most of us have imagined soaring with eagles, though few people take that daydream to the length my mom's mom did.

Two of her brothers—Al and Hubert—were well aware of Grandmom's flying fantasy, so they conspired together to come up with a good trick to tease their little sister. They told her that if she'd climb on top of the garage roof and eat an entire butterfly, she'd be able to soar like a bird. Of course, they knew that she was terrified of bugs, and they probably didn't think she'd actually go through with the dare.

They underestimated her burning desire to take wing.

Family legend has it that she gobbled both wings of the butterfly dangled in front of her and then inched to the edge of the roof, stretched out her arms, took a deep breath and jumped! Thank goodness she didn't break any bones, but Grandmom did learn that our world is governed by gravity. She also discovered that staying grounded is much less painful than "putting on airs"!

What's the *Story* of This Particular Book?

Nineveh, Assyria's capital city, had once responded with humility to Jonah-the-whale-rider's preaching, but at this point they had gotten way too big for their britches! You can sense Nahum's indignation when he points out their arrogance and spiritual rebellion in this prophecy. Furthermore, Nineveh is guilty of being a world-class bully with the nasty habit of beating up on other people groups—including God's chosen ones, the Israelites. It doesn't take much imagination to picture the divine comeuppance they're facing—they're about to take a really big fall!

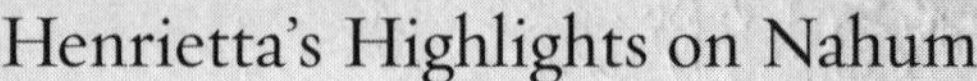

Henrietta's Highlights on Nahum

Her Synopsis
Jesus Christ, a Stronghold in the Day of Trouble

Her Suggested Bible Readings
Day One: *The Judge and the Verdict* (Nahum 1)
Day Two: *The Execution* (Nahum 2–3)

Memorable Quotes from Dr. Mears
"Deliverance for Judah, and destruction for her enemy Assyria, was God's great theme for His people."

"The message of Nahum shows what God can do with a wicked and rebellious people. He will utterly destroy them."

"The person or nation that deliberately and finally rejects God, deliberately and finally and fatally elects doom. Beware of this!"

Looking for Yourself in God's Love Story

1. The questions between the lines of this Minor Prophecy are: *Why does God allow the wicked to prosper? Why doesn't He just zap them the minute they misbehave?* When have questions like these run through your mind and why?

2. In the first chapter of Nahum, we read that God doesn't have a quick temper (see Nahum 1:3). How have you personally experienced God's patience?

Movie Clip Moment

The Ant Bully (2006) is a cute, animated, family movie with a moral. The bottom-line message is that being a bully is not cool. There are lots of teachable moments, but beware of the potty humor and a scene with a bare bottom!

Tenacious Trust in Really Tough Times

My best friend's dad, Michie (pronounced "Micky"), died recently. He was too young to die—too full of life, too much in love with his wife, too much fun as a father and grandfather. His death begs the question why God doesn't zap all the murderers and pedophiles instead of allowing men like Michie to get terminal cancer.

But I've never heard his wife, Michele Hill, question God. Not once. Not even when she held Michie's hand in the waning hours of his life. She had fallen in love with him when she was 17. They were together for more than 40 years, raised three wonderful kids and had countless Bible studies and barbeques in their home. I'll never forget her pointing toward his intensive care room and saying, "My favorite person in the whole wide world is right in there." Michele loved Thomas Michie Hill. But she loves God more.

When I visited them in the hospital the month before Michie passed away, Michele described an image God had given her. She said she saw Him with Michie under one arm and her under the other, and the Lord was wearing a cape. She said she thought it was odd that He was dressed in a cape—she had always imagined God wearing a robe—but then He whispered to her that He was wearing a cape so that nothing could come up from behind and take them by surprise. God assured her that anything that happened to them would have to look Him in the face first.

After describing that picture, Michele smiled, while tears streamed down her face. Then she said that she knew that *whatever* happened—whether Michie lived or died—God was in control. She was absolutely convinced of His gracious sovereignty. The sheer beauty of her unwavering trust in God's goodness despite her own grief left me speechless. I was amazed she could proclaim His faithfulness in the middle of a Lysol-scented waiting room.

Her confidence in God's mercy, regardless of what was going on around her, reminds me of the vow a tired Old Testament prophet made. His name is hard to pronounce, but his trust in God is unmistakable!

> Though the cherry trees don't blossom and the strawberries don't ripen,
> Though the apples are worm-eaten and the wheat fields stunted,
> Though the sheep pens are sheepless and the cattle barns empty,
> I'm singing joyful praise to God.
> I'm turning cartwheels of joy to my Savior God.
> Counting on God's rule to prevail,
> I take heart and gain strength
> (Habakkuk 3:17-19, *THE MESSAGE*).

What's the *Story* of This Particular Book?

Habakkuk's story takes place soon after "good" King Josiah was killed in battle. Remember, Josiah is the king who rediscovered God's Word and ushered in a season of spiritual renewal after the Israelites had effectively "lost" the Bible. However, following his death, God's people lost their groove and returned to their wild ways. That's why Habakkuk asks God—twice—why He doesn't simply wipe out the reprobates (see Habakkuk 1:2-4,12-13; 2:1). Habakkuk wonders if maybe God has fallen asleep behind the wheel! But God assures this earnest prophet, along with us, that He is *always* in control, regardless of what we see taking place around us. In short, human history follows a divine blueprint and this planet will never spin out of His sovereign authority. This information so encouraged Habakkuk that he ended his story with a song.

Henrietta's Highlights on Habakkuk

Her Synopsis
Jesus Christ, the God of My Salvation

Her Suggested Bible Readings
Day One: *Habakkuk's Complaint* (Habakkuk 1)
Day Two: *God's Reply* (Habakkuk 2)
Day Three: *Habakkuk's Song* (Habakkuk 3)

Memorable Quotes from Dr. Mears

"Habakkuk, in all his difficulties, went to God in prayer and waited patiently for His answer."

"Habakkuk asked his question of God. He did not call a committee or form a society to solve the problem of the day. He went straight to Jehovah and stated his problem."

"God cannot always give us a satisfactory answer, because our finite minds cannot grasp the thoughts of this infinite. His thoughts are high above our thoughts, and His ways above our ways (Isaiah 55:9), but we can trust God, always!"

Looking for Yourself in God's Love Story

1. Habakkuk 2:4 has been called the "anchor" verse of this book. And its significance is underscored several times in the New Testament (see Romans 1:17; Galatians 3:11; Hebrews 10:38). Compare and contrast the New Testament circumstances with what was going on when Habakkuk first penned those words.

2. What do you think Habakkuk and Jonah (the first *whale rider*) have in common? (Read Habakkuk 1:2-4 and Jonah 3:10–4 if you need a hint!)

3. When it comes to understanding God, what's the key difference in the descriptive terms "fair" and "just"?

4. When's the last time you posed a question similar to Habakkuk's—a moment when you wondered whether God was being "fair"?

Movie Clip Moment

C. S. Lewis is one of the most beloved Christian writers in history and is considered to be one of our most profound theologians. One of his most endearing qualities is his straightforward honesty. Some of his most influential works reflect a man wrestling with God—not unlike Habakkuk! Although he never seemed to *doubt* God's goodness, Mr. Lewis did trust Him enough to pose questions. I think his most poignant inquiries occurred after the death of his wife, Joy, which are recorded in the book *A Grief Observed* as well as in the movie *Shadowlands.* Sir Anthony Hopkins portrays a very believable Lewis and Debra Winger plays Joy with just enough spunk to not be pitiable or maudlin. *Shadowlands* is a beautifully acted true story about a brilliant—albeit flawed—Christian man who struggles to believe that God is *perfectly good*, even when life is horribly bad.

ZEPHANIAH

The Dance of the Delighted

My youngest nephew, John Michael, who is seven, is mad about guinea pigs. He really wanted a puppy, but when his parents repeatedly objected, my mom (his grandmother) just had to get the little guy *something*. She'd already bought him fish, so guinea pigs were the next logical step up the food-chain ladder—cuddlier than cold-blooded pets, but not as much work as a Labrador Retriever! Thus, "Patch" and "Patches" became part of the extended brood at my parent's home in Florida.

When I was visiting my family this summer, I spent one evening hanging out with John Michael while he frolicked with his furry friends. He danced in circles around them, "chatted" nose to nose with them and stretched out on the floor so the pseudo-rats could scurry around on his tummy. The entire time, he kept erupting into contagious giggles!

My nephew wasn't doing anything particularly praiseworthy—he wasn't doing his homework, he wasn't doing his chores, he wasn't reciting poetry—he was simply doing what he loves to do during this season of his little-boy life, and that's playing with two guinea pigs. But I don't think I could have enjoyed him more if he'd just won the National Spelling Bee or composed a symphony!

It's taken me a very long time to believe that God delights in me, even when I'm just *being me*. I used to think God was a stern taskmaster and the only time He was pleased with me was when I was doing something "religious," like volunteering with children's Sunday School or teaching the Bible at a women's conference. Basically I thought He loved me out of *duty*—because it was written in His divine job description. The concept of God's *delighting* in me seemed as plausible as pigs flying (actually I can imagine John Michael's *guinea* pigs taking flight—if he felt the need to launch them!).

But this petite book named after a minor prophet actually records that eye-popping promise: "The LORD your God is with you, he is mighty to save. He will take great delight in you, he will quiet you with his love, he will rejoice over you with singing" (Zephaniah 3:17). Even though God's people were behaving badly, even though they deserved a big fat spanking, our merciful Creator chose to sing lyrics of restoration. Instead of knocking them across the room, He crooned a love song. And that kind of music makes me feel like dancing!

What's the *Story* of This Particular Book?

While the "poster verse" of Zephaniah paints a picture of God singing over us, the overall theme of this book is that God will not compromise His holiness. God won't wink at sin. Yet during this period of ancient history, His people—the Israelites—were rebelling like there was no tomorrow. God's kids had gone so wild they literally lost the Bible (see 2 Kings 22:3-13 for the whole story). So Zephaniah warns them to get their act together and then prophesies about a "remnant" who won't sully themselves with sin and who will seek refuge in God.

Henrietta's Highlights on Zephaniah

Her Synopsis
Zephaniah Portrays Jesus Christ, a Jealous Lord

Her Suggested Bible Readings
Day One: *Coming Judgments* (Zephaniah 1–2)
Day Two: *The Kingdom Blessings* (Zephaniah 3)

Memorable Quotes from Dr. Mears
"As you start reading this book, you are appalled at its contents. There is nothing but denunciations, dire threats and wrath. Cowper (William Cowper, 1731-1800, British poet and hymn writer) says that punishment and chastisement is the 'graver countenance of love.' 'For whom the Lord loveth he chasteneth, and scourgeth every son whom he receiveth' (Hebrews 12:6). We see in all this a proof of God's love. The book begins with sorrow, but ends with singing."

"The Jews taught that Jerusalem was the place of worship. The Samaritans declared that Mount Gerizim ought to be the religious center, but Zephaniah taught that spiritual worship did not depend on a place, but on the Presence of God."

"The rejoicing of Zephaniah 3:14-20 must refer to something besides the day when the remnant will return after the captivity of Babylon . . . It must refer to the day when the Lord Himself shall sit on the throne of David, when His people shall be gathered from the four corners of the earth (3:19)."

Looking for Yourself in God's Love Story

1. What was the occasion of the most serious spanking (or other form of discipline) you received as a child? What "spiritual spanking"—discipline that was clearly from God—has taught you the biggest lesson?

2. Read Zephaniah 1:4-6, Deuteronomy 4:19 and Jeremiah 8:2. Some people—including Christians—think reading their horoscope in a newspaper or magazine is completely harmless. What do you think?

3. Read Zephaniah 1:17. How would you describe the relationship between disobedience and spiritual blindness? Have you ever felt like you were *groping*—distanced from God—because of bad choices?

4. Read Zephaniah 3:9-11. Some people think these verses apply only to the Israelites. But then why in verse 9 would God say He'll change the speech of the "peoples" (the original Hebrew denoted plurality, or more than one people group)? Do you think He might be referring to a multicultural *remnant*? If so, how would you describe the "color and culture" of heaven?

Movie Clip Moment

Morgan Freeman is one of my favorite actors—I loved him in *Driving Miss Daisy*, *Glory* and *The Shawshank Redemption*. I also like the character he portrays in a film titled *Lean on Me*, which was based on the true story of a maverick high school principal named Joe Clark. Mr. Clark was hired to take over the notorious Eastside High in New Jersey. When he assumed leadership, drug dealers and gang members ruled the hallways and terrorized the teachers. Morgan Freeman—playing Principal Clark—initiates a "war" against the thugs to take back the school they've hijacked, and it soon becomes crystal clear that he has absolutely no patience for hoodlums—he refuses to let troublemakers destroy Eastside High and the good students who are there to learn. This reminds me of how God refused to let sin reign any longer in Israel. He loves His children too much to sit idly on His throne while their sinfulness spirals out of control. And there's no way He will allow out-of-control sin to poison our hope in Him.

An Inconvenient Faith

This past Christmastime, my trusty old washing machine started spitting and sputtering—I decided it was about time to get a new one. While I was shopping the circulars, I thought, "I might as well get a new dryer too, because mine's ancient and that way I'll have a matching set" (as if anyone but me would even walk into the laundry room to admire them!).

But once I began making comparison shopping trips to appliance stores, I was overwhelmed into indecision by the dazzling array of washing and drying "systems" to choose from. They now come in a rainbow of colors. They offer steam-cleaning options and have special attachments for washing unique items (like tennis shoes). The dryers are equipped with computer sensors that weigh the laundry so that you aren't inconvenienced by having to lift a finger and press a button. These fancy new machines are the ultimate in user-friendly—they can do just about everything except fold the clothes (which would be great!).

I think lots of people are shopping for a spiritual system that's user-friendly. They'd like to listen to short, engaging sermons that can be downloaded on their iPod, because actually attending services is a scheduling nuisance. They'd prefer inspirational topics, because they've got enough stress at work without having to think about controversial topics like how touchy God is about sin. They also don't want to bother with any financial support for the church, because they assume religious entities are funded by some federal slush fund anyway. Besides, they have to save their cash for cool metallic cleaning machines.

Most people want a relationship with God that doesn't require any hassle on their part. Dietrich Bonhoeffer lamented our quest for "easy faith" well when he wrote:

> Cheap grace is the preaching of forgiveness without requiring repentance, baptism without church discipline, Communion without confession, absolution without

> personal confession. Cheap grace is grace without discipleship, grace without the cross, grace without Jesus Christ, living and incarnate.[3]

In other words, Christ's blood wasn't shed so that we could have cushy lives.

What's the *Story* of This Particular Book?

Haggai wrote this wake-up call because after a brief attempt at rebuilding the Temple in Jerusalem (this is one of three "post-exilic" books–along with Zechariah and Malachi–that were recorded after the Israelites returned home from captivity in Babylon), the Israelites had given up. They decided the Temple project was just too difficult, so instead of buckling down and fixing God's house, they took a shopping trip to Home Depot and started sprucing up their own private residences. The result of their "walkout" was an immediate decline in worship–now they didn't have a sanctuary in which to express their devotion! Therefore, God tells Haggai to get a megaphone and charge His people to grab their hardhats and hammers and get their behinds back to the Temple where they belong!

Henrietta's Highlights on Haggai

Her Synopsis
Jesus Christ, the Desire of All Nations

Her Suggested Bible Readings
Day One: *Haggai's Message* (Haggai 1–2)

Memorable Quote from Dr. Mears
"This book is dominated by one central purpose: Haggai is determined to persuade the people to rebuild the Temple. It is no easy task to move a discouraged nation to rise up and build a temple. But he did it."

Looking for Yourself in God's Love Story

Read Haggai 1:5-7,12-13. How would you describe the relationship between *contrition* and *seeing God clearly*?

Movie Clip Moment

The best movie I've ever seen that highlights the gold at the end of the rainbow of inconvenience is called *Secondhand Lions.* This heartwarming story illustrates how greatness is defined by following through on lifetime commitments, in spite of hassles and difficulties of all kinds. Young Walter (played by Haley Joel Osment) is forced to spend the summer with his crotchety bachelor uncles (played by Sir Michael Caine and Robert Duvall), who are beyond put out by his arrival. The ensuing relational fireworks are comical and, ultimately, very touching. With the exception of a few expletives, this is a great family flick!

Put Some Zing in Your Thing

My mom has a pretty refined vocabulary—she was raised Baptist, so saying bad words isn't in her communicatory repertoire. I've only heard her spout a mild expletive once in my whole life, and that was only after we kids had stretched her patience to the absolute limit.

It happened when we were supposed to be helping her around the house. I don't remember exactly what chore she'd asked us to complete—probably cleaning the garage or mowing the lawn—but it was hot and my brother and I were much more interested in lounging than laboring. So we dabbled at our work and then dove into the pool to cool off.

We were splashing and squealing, oblivious to anything but our own entertainment, when Mom came stomping around the corner. She stalked up to the edge of our watery refuge and then—with hands firmly on her hips—called my brother and me, using our full names (you know you're in big trouble when your mom uses your middle name). When we sheepishly paddled over to where she stood, she delivered an impassioned speech about responsibility and work ethic and starving children in Africa. Then she shocked us both by using the term "half-assed" to describe the job we'd done. We knew better than to grin or giggle during her outburst, but I sure get tickled now at the thought of my very appropriate but exasperated mother blurting out that close-to-cussing word!

What's the *Story* of This Particular Book?

My mom's colorful modifier is an apt description of how the Israelites were rebuilding the Temple. As they did in Haggai's time, they'd lost interest in the chore of working on God's house and snuck back to their own neighborhoods to watch soap operas and redecorate their personal residences. So Jehovah appointed this motivational prophet named Zechariah to preach an "If You Build

It, He Will Come" message to remind the lazy Israelites of their Messiah's imminent return. Zechariah's inspirational sermon series jumpstarted a flurry of activity and interest, causing the Temple project to be completed in just four years (516 B.C.)!

Henrietta's Highlights on Zechariah

Her Synopsis
Jesus Christ, the Righteous Branch

Her Suggested Bible Readings
Day One: *Visions* (Zechariah 1–6)
Day Two: *Fasts* (Zechariah 7–8)
Day Three: *Restoration of Judah and Israel* (Zechariah 9–11)
Day Four: *The Messiah* (Zechariah 12–14)

Memorable Quotes from Dr. Mears
"Zechariah, a young prophet who had stood alongside the aged Haggai, strengthened the children of Israel as they built the Temple and warned them not to disappoint God as their fathers had done."

"Zechariah does not condemn the people, but presents in glowing pictures the presence of God to strengthen and help."

Looking for Yourself in God's Love Story

1. Read Zechariah 3:8; 9:9,16; 11:11-13; 12:10; 13:1,6-7; 14. Zechariah is second only to Isaiah with regard to specific prophecies about Jesus. Which of the above images is your favorite and why?

2. Zechariah's ancient story brings up an obvious question for us today: Do you put as much effort and passion into projects for *God's glory* as you do in projects geared to reward *you* personally?

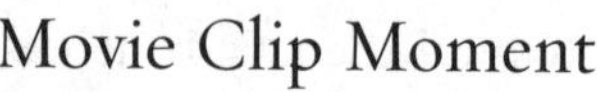

Movie Clip Moment

This one was a no-brainer from the beginning–I simply have to recommend the 1989 baseball movie *Field of Dreams*! While Ray Kinsella's (played by Kevin Costner) fictional mission to build a baseball diamond in a cornfield is more fanciful than the Israelite's historical quest to rebuild the Temple on a hill in Jerusalem, they share a similar motivation: "If You Build It, They Will Come." Kevin Costner hopes his childhood baseball heroes will come walking out of the cornstalks when he completes his project. God's people hope the Messiah will split the sky to inhabit His earthly residence when they complete theirs.

MALACHI

When Everything That Could Go Wrong Does

I have a tendency to question God's goodness during difficult seasons. Sometimes His grace seems less than amazing when my life is less than I'd hoped for. I had one of those whining, doubting days a few years ago on the Fourth of July.

I was in the middle of a breakup with a man I'd fallen in love with, so I went over to my best friend Kim's house to take my mind off him. I was in her garage installing shelves when the ladder I was perched on slipped and crashed to the cement floor, 12 feet below. I was only knocked out for a few seconds and was pretty sure I wasn't hurt too badly, but the goose egg over my eye and the copious amount of blood prompted Kim to ask me a series of worried questions: What's your full name? What's your address? What's today's date? Who's the president?

Kim insisted that we go to the hospital, but I really didn't want to be in the ER all night with a bunch of drunks who had barbecued their fingers with fireworks. And while I was playing the belligerent patient to Kim's trauma nurse, something much worse than my fall occurred.

My little dog, Reba (don't ask, I didn't name her!), who had been left outside next to the fence during the mishap, got tangled up in her leash and died. I still get teary thinking about it—and I'm not even one of those people who wears a T-shirt featuring my pet's picture. It was awful; Kim went outside to get her and came back with a dazed look. When she told me Reba was dead, I was still woozy, so I thought maybe I'd misunderstood her. I asked Kim to repeat herself, and then—because the news was so unbelievably awful—I asked if she was teasing.

"No, Reba's really dead," Kim said, and then she started to laugh hysterically. It wasn't *happy* laughter either, more like wearing-a-straightjacket-in-a-room-with-padded-walls laughter. Kim is typically a very steady, logical person, but finding me sprawled out on the garage floor covered in blood and then finding Reba in the first stages of rigor mortis had wreaked havoc on her typically calm demeanor.

To top it all off, after taking Reba to the vet to be "disposed of," Kim had a hair appointment with the same guy who had given me the dog. He loved that terrier much more than I ever did—he had asked me to take her only because his kids were allergic to dog hair and his wife had put her foot down. Thus, when Kim got to the salon and told him about Reba's accident, he was devastated. He responded by telling her he'd just had sinus surgery and couldn't blow his nose—he tilted his head back and excused himself from the room. He had several more grieving, tilting moments during Kim's haircut, and she came back looking like she'd lost an argument with a weed wacker.

Let me tell you, that Independence Day was a really, really bad day!

The Israelites certainly knew what it was like to have bad days. By the end of the Old Testament, they'd suffered a very long season of bad days, and their disappointment showed like a dirty slip.

> God said, "I love you." You replied, "Really? How have you loved us?" (Malachi 1:2, *THE MESSAGE*).

The Paul Harvey part of this story reveals God comforting these stinkers instead of spanking them into submission. Even though they have doubted Him, God delights to give them mercy. And thankfully, He's still in the business of extending grace to His griping children today!

What's the *Story* of This Particular Book?

Malachi is the last book of a 12-book section at the end of the Old Testament called the Minor Prophets. It's the last time we hear God's recorded voice for almost 400 years (the *Intertestamental Period*, more commonly known as The Silent Years), until another prophet named John the Baptist starts talking. Malachi's story takes place just as the first wave of Israelites are returning to their hometown of Jerusalem after a long, hard season of captivity in Babylon (basically a divine time-out from God to discipline them for their rebellious ways). But instead of finding Israel the Land of Milk and Honey that they had left, they discover that their beloved birthplace has turned into a great big mess. The walls surrounding the once-great city are in ruins, their homes have been burned, their businesses ransacked, and their fertile fields now lie in ruins. Rather than acknowledge the consequences of their rebellion, they begin to grumble and complain and blame God for their problems. Even their religious leaders misbehave and shake their fists at Jehovah. It's a wonder that God didn't just zap them all into oblivion!

Henrietta's Highlights on Malachi

Her Synopsis
Jesus Christ, Son of Righteousness

Her Suggested Bible Readings
Day One: *Sins of Priests and People* (Malachi 1–2)
Day Two: *Message of Hope* (Malachi 3–4)

Memorable Quotes from Dr. Mears
"Martin Luther called John 3:16 'the little gospel.' In the same way, we might speak of Malachi as the 'little Old Testament.'"

"The skeptical attitude aroused among the people showed itself in religious coldness and social laxity. This is always true."

"The children of Israel could depend on Jehovah to forgive. It was this same picture of the Father Jesus gave when He told of the prodigal's return. The father, seeing the boy while yet a great way off, ran out to meet him. This is ever God's attitude."

Looking for Yourself in God's Love Story

1. Does the thought of God's all-seeing, all-knowing presence fill you with comfort or anxiety? Explain why.

2. Read Malachi 1:6-7,11-14 and Proverbs 3:9-10. What would giving God the "first fruits" of your attention and affection look like? Do you find it harder to part with money or time?

3. Read Psalm 119:75; Jeremiah 9:7-11,23-24; Zechariah 13:8-9; Malachi 2:17–3:5. What would you say is the recurring theme in these passages? What adjectives would you use to describe God's discipline?

4. Do you think the process of being "purified" by God always involves pain?

Movie Clip Moment

I can't help but associate the storyline of Malachi with the mother of all Southern-belle movies, *Gone with the Wind.* You probably remember Margaret Mitchell's infamous heroine, Scarlett O'Hara (played by actress Vivien Leigh), and the tantrums she throws when things don't go her way! I'll never forget her hoop skirts, "fiddle-dee-dee" phrase or how she creates couture out of velvet curtains, but I think the most memorable scene in the movie takes place when she stands defiantly in what's left of their garden—everything had been ravaged by the Civil War—raises her fist to the sky and declares, "With God as my witness, I'll never be hungry again." Spunky Scarlett had returned home to find her beloved Tara (the name of their plantation) trashed, much like when the first wave of Israelites return home to find Canaan completely destroyed and their beloved Temple lying in ruins. Both Scarlett's and Malachi's peers raise their fists to the heavens. Both wonder, *If God is so good, then why are our lives so bad?* The common denominator in their stories is selfish discontent.

A Tale of Two Gardens

Jesus cries in the Garden of Gethsemane. He sheds real tears when contemplating His death on a cross. He doesn't square His shoulders and stoically encounter death like the Christian martyrs who will come after Him. No, Christ's sacrifice on Calvary is completely different than a martyr's death. It may sound like I'm splitting hairs here, but there is a significant difference between the guts of a martyr and the grief Jesus experiences in that grove of olive trees. The big difference is in *Who* is doing the persecuting.

God is the one putting Jesus to death. Christ's courage isn't in question; it's not an issue of valor. Jesus could have called in legions of angels to rescue Him from the Roman soldiers and the angry mob of Jewish citizens. He could have grabbed a sword and, like Peter, started slicing off ears to make His point. Or He could have simply vaporized everyone with just one breath. No, Christ's anguish didn't have anything to do with a lack of nerve. Jesus wasn't afraid—He was brokenhearted. Our Redeemer wept because He knew He would be separated from God the Father, the very moment He took our sins on His shoulders.

He wasn't surprised when the disciples betrayed Him and scattered. They were already down to 11 anyway. He was well aware that He'd be by Himself in the dark days leading up to His death, bereft of the companionship and support of His followers. Even his dear, hotheaded friend Peter—who had vowed to stay with Him until death—would get scared and run away. Jesus could handle all that; He was used to being alone here on Earth. But He'd never experienced being estranged from God. He'd never looked in the eyes of His Father and seen wrath.

God began human history—*His* story—in an altogether different garden. A place called Eden, a wonderful place where Adam and Eve existed in perfect relationship with their Creator. Things were as they were made to be. But then Eve got deceived by a slithery jerk, who encouraged her to eat some rotten fruit, which ruined the relationship between God and humanity. Separation crept in with the snake. In that first garden, humans messed up royally by saying to God, "Not Your will, but mine." God told humanity not to eat that particular produce and we replied, "I'm gonna eat it anyway because I want to!" Ever since, we've been saying the same thing: "I wanna do things my way!"

God sets the stage to complete human history—again *His* story—in Gethsemane. In that garden, Jesus (whom the apostle Paul calls the "second Adam") atones for original sin. In the second garden, Jesus says, "Not my will, but Yours be done." Jesus endures the full fury and rejection of God that sin deserves so that we can be reconciled with Him. Jesus pays the highest price possible so that we can reconnect with our Creator. He cries out, "My God, my God, why have You forsaken me?" so that we won't ever have to say it—or feel it. Martyrdom didn't put Jesus on the cross—*mercy* did.

What's the *Story* of This Particular Book?

Reading the four Gospels is like listening to four different people who are standing on four different street corners describe a parade that's passing by—they all have unique perspectives and viewpoints! Matthew is the first of the four Gospel writers, and the flavor of his writing is one that would appeal to a Jewish audience. He emphasizes the *revelation* of King Jesus, the *rebellion* against King Jesus, the *retirement* of King Jesus, the *rejection* of King Jesus and the *resurrection* of King Jesus. Furthermore, Matthew's narrative is *thematic*—he tells Jesus' story in big colorful chunks instead of chronologically like Mark and Luke. (The first three Gospel accounts—Matthew, Mark and Luke—are formally called the Synoptic Gospels, which means "taken together" and denotes their relatively similar style and format).

Henrietta's Highlights on Matthew

Her Synopsis

Matthew Portrays Jesus Christ, The Promised Messiah

Her Suggested Bible Readings

Sunday: *The King Born* (Matthew 1:18–2:23)
Monday: *The King Begins Work* (Matthew 4)
Tuesday: *The King States Kingdom Laws* (Matthew 5:1-17,38-48; 6:19-34)
Wednesday: *The King and His Followers* (Matthew 10:1-33)
Thursday: *The Kingdom Mysteries* (Matthew 13:1-52)
Friday: *The King Offers Himself as King* (Matthew 21:1-11)
Saturday: *The King Will Return* (Matthew 25:14-30)

Memorable Quotes from Dr. Mears

"Matthew links us up with the Old Testament. On every page he is trying to connect the Gospel with the prophets and show that all of their teaching is being fulfilled in the person and kingdom of Jesus Christ."

"The wise men were led to a Person, not a creed."

"'But whom say ye that I am?' Ask yourself this question . . . No one can escape it. A neutral answer is impossible. He is either God or an imposter."

"Jesus was slain because He claimed to be the King of Israel. He was raised from the dead because He was the King."

"After hanging on the cruel tree for six hours, the Savior died, not from physical suffering alone but of a broken heart, for He bore the sins of the whole world."

Looking for Yourself in God's Love Story

1. The word "gospel" literally means "good news." When do you first remember hearing about the good news of God's love for you? How did you respond initially?

2. What are some of the more humiliating things you think Jesus submitted to in becoming a man? What adjectives would you use to describe the journey from King of kings to being nailed through the wrists and feet on a wooden cross, and then dying in front of a jeering crowd?

3. Read the Sermon on the Mount (see Matthew 5–7). Why do you think *poverty* and *meekness* aren't really considered virtues in our culture? How would you explain their value to an unbeliever?

4. The Sermon on the Mount seems to emphasize the Law of God—where do you see *grace* in this message?

Movie Clip Moment

Several years ago I went to see a movie called *The Spitfire Grill.* It wasn't a big budget film—I don't remember ever even seeing an advertisement for it. There were no special effects or eye-popping computer-generated imagery. But it was one of the best movies I've ever seen. The main character, a young woman named Percy Talbot (played by actress Alison Elliott) is released from prison and moves to a small town named Gilead, in Maine. I won't spoil the storyline by saying any more—suffice it to say, if you choose to rent *The Spitfire Grill*, you'll find yourself sitting on the edge of the couch thoroughly engaged in this modern morality tale! And you'll have a much better understanding of what meekness looks like after watching it.

MARK

Shallow Jerks in Sheep's Clothing

Several years ago I met someone who reminded me that simply *attending* Christian events doesn't make you Christlike, any more than sitting in McDonalds makes you a hamburger!

This reminder took place when I was on a business trip in Texas. After overindulging in Mexican food all week, I decided I needed to lose a few pounds fast or the clothes I'd packed were going to cut off my circulation! I had literally gotten too big for my britches. So I went for a workout in the fitness center and exercised energetically, hoping for major shrinkage.

After a short season of straining and regretting my deep affection for chips and salsa, I walked back to the lobby to wait for the elevator to take me back to my room so that I could get ready for a banquet that evening. When the doors opened, there stood an impeccably dressed woman, dripping with gold jewelry and elegance. Her suit was beautiful and her hair—like everything else in Texas—was big. (Luckily I'm not a smoker, because one lit match and the hairspray in there would have blown up the hotel.)

Since we were the only people on the elevator and were headed to the same floor, I tried to engage her in conversation. I can't remember exactly what I said—probably something about the weather. But she didn't respond; she stared straight ahead and completely ignored me. I thought, *Oh, no, poor thing must be hard of hearing.* So I leaned in closer with a big grin and repeated my comment much louder, intent on connecting with the dear, deaf lady. Only this time, she glanced pointedly and irritably out of the corner of her eye and then stared back at the blinking lights on the elevator panel and exhaled *very* loudly as if to say, "You're sweaty and stinky and don't deserve my company." Needless to say, I was flustered and embarrassed. When the doors finally opened on our floor, she brushed past me haughtily and walked away without so much as a backward glance.

About an hour later, after I'd showered and slathered on makeup and squeezed into a fancy suit myself, I headed up to the hotel ballroom to hostess an invitation-only event for an international ministry. The room was packed with well-dressed, wealthy patrons and—much to my surprise—the condescending elevator chick! When the program was over and I stepped down from the platform, she sashayed over to greet me. Then she gushed like some melodramatic Scarlett O'Hara, "Eye wee-ush you had tole me who you wer-uh on the elah-va-tore . . . beecuz eye would have luuuved to have tawlked to you if only eye'd known who you wer-uh!"

All I could think of in reply was, *And I wish I could kick you right in the shins, snotty!* (But I kept my mouth shut.)

Some religious people are just downright difficult to love, aren't they? Some people look pious on the outside yet have nasty, petty little hearts on the inside. This is the assessment Jesus makes about quite a few church leaders in His day:

> As he taught, Jesus said, "Watch out for the teachers of the law. They like to walk around in flowing robes and be greeted in the marketplaces, and have the most important seats in the synagogues and the places of honor at banquets. They devour widows' houses and for a show make lengthy prayers. Such men will be punished most severely" (Mark 12:38-40).

Yikes—it sounds like people who are more concerned with *looking spiritual* than with *loving God* better shape up or else they're headed for a really painful supernatural spanking!

What's the *Story* of This Particular Book?

Mark's message is a declaration of *good news* for the whole world! His narrative picks up at the launch of Jesus' public ministry and highlights how He meets human needs. Mark's style includes more of a sense of urgency than the other Gospel accounts do. For example, he uses the word "immediately" about 40 times—making his account feel more like an action flick than a documentary! Mark also underscores Jesus' humanity, describing Him sleeping (see Mark 4:38) and hungry (see Mark 11:12). Interestingly enough, some scholars believe that Mark's Gospel is actually a secondhand account of Peter's firsthand experiences with the Messiah. (Peter was the person who led Mark to Christ.)

Henrietta's Highlights on Mark

Her Synopsis
Mark Portrays Jesus Christ, the Servant of God

Her Suggested Bible Readings

Sunday: *The Servant's Coming and Testing* (Mark 1:1-20)
Monday: *The Servant Working* (Mark 2:1–3:25)
Tuesday: *The Servant Speaking* (Mark 4:1–6:13)
Wednesday: *The Servant's Miracles* (Mark 6:32–8:26)
Thursday: *The Servant's Revelation* (Mark 8:27–10:34)
Friday: *The Servant's Rejection* (Mark 11–12)
Saturday: *The Servant's Death and Triumph* (Mark 14–16)

Memorable Quotes from Dr. Mears

"Unlike Matthew, Mark was not trying to prove certain statements and prophecies concerning Jesus. His only object in writing was to tell clearly certain facts about Jesus. His deeds more especially than His words."

"One of the first things that impresses us as we look at Mark's Gospel is its brevity . . . It moves off with precision."

"Jesus silenced His enemies, but their hearts would not yield. Then He exposed all their hypocritical practices in words that fell like bombs."

"Jesus was sold for thirty pieces of silver, the price of a slave. He was executed as only slaves were! Yes, Christ was the suffering Servant and died for me! He bore my sins in His own body on the tree."

Looking for Yourself in God's Love Story

1. Read Acts 13–15. Contrast the immaturity that handicapped Mark (see Acts 15:36-41) early in his walk of faith with the wisdom he displays in his Gospel.

2. Read Mark 4:35–5. This passage points to Jesus' omnipotence by describing His lordship in four unique situations. Can you find the four distinct things He was victorious over in these verses?

3. Read Mark 14:3-9. What's the costliest thing you've ever given Jesus?

Movie Clip Moment

Although this movie infuriated conservatives across the country when it was released, I still think adult believers should watch *Saved!* in the privacy of their own homes. This film affords us a glimpse of how many people stereotype Christians. And while it's certainly an unflattering perspective, it's also an all-too-often accurate opinion. We *do* tend to focus on moralistic behavior rather than admitting our desperate need for God's mercy. We *are* prone to criticize prodigals instead of extending compassion to them. We *can* get testy about religion more than we testify about our relationship with Jesus. We *could* use a big serving of humble pie!

The Paul Harvey Part of God's Story

I heard a story today about a man, a bird, a fox and a cow. Well, sort of a cow. It went something like this: Once upon a time a man was walking from his farmhouse to the village when he happened upon a baby bird that had fallen from its nest. It was a cold day and the bird seemed to be near death, so the man scooped up the swallow and cupped it in his hands. As he was standing there, anxious about missing his appointment in town and pondering what to do with the wee bird, he noticed a fresh cow pie at the edge of the road.

He thought, *It's soft and warm . . . it just might work.* So he gingerly placed the little bird in the middle of a new "nest." He watched over the bird for a few minutes until it began to show signs of reviving. When it began to sing, the man smiled and continued on his journey whistling, thinking he'd just saved a swallow. However, a fox that was patrolling the very same pasture had also heard the song. He waited for the man to disappear over the hill, and then snatched the bird out of the pie for a midmorning snack.

The moral of the story is that the one who got you into a mess isn't necessarily your enemy, the one who gets you out isn't necessarily your friend, and whenever you find yourself up to your neck in a mess, it behooves you to keep your mouth shut!

In the Gospels, a story that conveys moral points, or spiritual principles, is called a *parable*, and Jesus told a lot of them. As a matter of fact, approximately one-third of the Synoptic Gospels (Matthew, Mark and Luke) are parables! And while parables can be gripping, they can also be problematic. Sometimes the meaning is difficult to interpret. Sometimes the context is confusing. Sometimes the characters are less than sympathetic. Sometimes it's hard to tell exactly where *you* fit into the story!

Theologians teach that Jesus used these sometimes perplexing tales to engage those who were interested and to push away those who didn't believe. Many who heard Him responded, "These are stupid stories that don't make any sense, so I'm outta here because I've got better things to do." However, a few stayed. They were compelled by the things Christ said and wanted to know more. They leaned in to listen longer because they *just had to hear* the Paul Harvey part of God's story!

In parable terminology, those who hung on Jesus' words had hearts filled with fertile soil, where grace could grow. But those who walked away disinterested had hearts filled with rocks and thorns, where nothing grew. What kind of dirt is filling up your chest? Are you a *listener* or a *leaver*?

What's the *Story* of This Particular Book?

Author Luke was probably the only non-Jewish person to write a book in the Bible. He was also a medical doctor, which explains the themes of compassion and healing that permeate his perspective on Jesus' life and ministry. Furthermore, there's a theme of universality in Luke—stories about Christ's interactions with women, children and Samaritans—highlighting the fact that Immanuel came to save *all* humankind, not just the Jews. His Birth narrative is the most richly detailed and is the one you're most likely to hear at the annual church Christmas production! And, of course, the book of Luke includes more parables than either Matthew or Mark.

Henrietta's Highlights on Luke

Her Synopsis
Luke Portrays Jesus Christ, the Son of Man

Her Suggested Bible Readings

Sunday: *The Man "Made Like unto His Brethren"* (Luke 1–3)
Monday: *The Man "Tempted Like as We Are"* (Luke 4:1–8:3)
Tuesday: *The Man "Touched with . . . Our Infirmities"* (Luke 8:4–12:48)
Wednesday: *The Man "About My Father's Business"* (Luke 12:49–16)
Thursday: *The Man "Never Man Spake Like This Man"* (Luke 17:1–19:27)

Friday: *The Man, Our Kinsman-Redeemer* (Luke 19:28–23)
Saturday: *The Man in Resurrection Glory* (Luke 24)

Memorable Quotes from Dr. Mears
"This is the Gospel for the sinner. It brings out Christ's compassionate love in becoming man to save man."

"Luke is the Gospel for the outcast on earth. It is Luke who tells of the Good Samaritan (10:33), the publican (18:13), and the prodigal (15:11-24), of Zacchaeus (19:2) and the thief on the cross (23:43)."

"He is the writer who has the most to say for womanhood (chapters 1 and 2)."

"The more you crush a rose, the more its fragrance is recognized. So the more the devil assaults Christ, the more will His perfections be revealed."

Looking for Yourself in God's Love Story

1. Read Luke 1:1-4. How would you summarize Luke's *purpose* for writing this Gospel account?

2. One of the key words/themes that come up over and over in Luke is Christ's *compassion*. How have you sensed God's extending compassion toward you recently?

3. Read Luke 14 and 15. Both chapters describe Jesus' associations with colorful characters and are thus sometimes called the "party parables." With whom do you think Jesus would most often associate in our culture? Do you think the Christians you know would approve or disapprove of Jesus' relationships?

4. Read Luke 24:13-35. Luke is the only Gospel that records this account of Christ's appearance—after His crucifixion and resurrection, but before His ascension—to a couple of bewildered disciples on the Emmaus

Road. It's a wonderful story about how Jesus patiently tutored two guys who didn't even recognize Him! What relationships and/or situations tend to distract you from really *seeing* Jesus?

Movie Clip Moment

It is unquestionably the most successful Christ-centered film of all times, and *The Passion of the Christ* is also unflinchingly realistic. It portrays both the Incarnate aspect—Jesus was perfectly human and perfectly divine at the same time—of our Messiah, as well as His tangible mercy for mistake-prone people like us. And the crucifixion scene, while emotionally disturbing, affirms that only a supernatural, unconditional love for humanity could compel God to allow His only Son to suffer like that. Watching Christ's great compassion for us so vividly dramatized should surely stir humility and gratitude in our feeble hearts.

Bigger Than a Breadbox

I heard a true story recently about a kindergarten Sunday School class. It was the Sunday before Easter and the teacher wanted to remind her students of what Easter was really all about, so she began class with a question to help them to understand that many of the holidays we celebrate are really about Jesus. She asked her crew of five- and six-year-olds if anyone could explain the meaning of Christmas. One little boy raised his hand and said, "It's when Jesus became incarnate and all the angels sang and the shepherds worshiped and the wise men came."

The teacher said, "That was an excellent answer, Billy," thinking to herself, *His parents must be teachers or something.* Then she asked, "And who can tell me about Palm Sunday?"

Billy raised his hand again and announced, "It's when Jesus entered Jerusalem as the Messiah and all the people laid down palm branches and it was the beginning of the last week of His life."

By now, the teacher was very impressed—maybe even a little intimidated! She looked around the room, smiling encouragement at the other children, and then asked, "Now can anyone else explain the significance of Good Friday?" A few moments passed and the kids started shifting nervously in their seats.

When it became obvious that no one else was going to speak, she nodded at the budding scholar who solemnly declared, "That's when Jesus was crucified on a cross for our sins and the Temple curtain was ripped in half and He gave up His spirit to God the Father."

The teacher smiled and said, "Why don't you just go ahead and tell us about Easter, Billy."

At which point young William sat up straighter in his chair, cleared his throat and proudly proclaimed, "That's when Jesus came out of the tomb, but then He saw His shadow, so He went back inside for another six weeks."

I've met a lot of people—even in the middle of the "Bible Belt"—who resemble that little guy. People who go to church most Sundays and know a lot *about* God—but like Billy, they get some of the core issues confused. Typically, they either caricaturize Him as a sort of supernatural Santa Claus whose main role is to give them the presents on their wish list, or they vilify God as a kind of divine Darth Vader who's out to get them—either an overly indulgent "favorite uncle" figure or a harsh disciplinarian bent on squeezing the joy out of our lives. But God defies both of those stereotypes. He is infinitely more compassionate than some jolly childhood cartoon and much more awe-inspiring than a light saber-wielding asthmatic in a metal mask and black cape.

The most brilliant theological minds of history have never come up with a definition that adequately captures God. He is beyond human description. He is perfect love with imperfect people; He embraces lepers and befriends prostitutes. He is a consuming fire—so altogether holy and fearsome that we couldn't look directly at Him if He were to appear in our midst.

The apostle John, one of three men who enjoyed the closest relationships with Jesus here on Earth, paints a beautiful portrait of God's complexity. John talks of leaning against the breast of Jesus—he literally felt the beat of Immanuel's heart (see John 13:21-25; 21:20). Dear John also says that when he experienced a vision of Jesus glorified, he was so overwhelmed that he fainted (see Revelation 1:9-20)!

God chose to become a spotless Lamb, led to the slaughter to pay for our sins, and He reigns over all the earth as the omnipotent, all-powerful Lion of Judah. He certainly doesn't fit in the mental boxes we create for Him!

What's the *Story* of This Particular Book?

John's Gospel account varies quite a bit from the style of the three Synoptic Gospels. He shares a few unique observations, such as when Jesus turned ordinary tap water into award-winning wine to avert a wedding-party disaster (see John 2:1-10); when Jesus poignantly raised His stinky friend Lazarus from the dead (see John 11:1-44); and how Jesus lovingly "discipled" the disciples to prepare them for His death and resurrection (see John 13–14). He also uses different phraseology to describe our Messiah, calling Him both the "Word of God" and the "Lamb of God." And John's theme is decidedly *evangelistic*—in other words, his purpose and passion in writing this book was that people would read about Jesus and *believe*!

Henrietta's Highlights on John

Her Synopsis
John Portrays Jesus Christ, the Son of God

Her Suggested Bible Readings

Sunday: *Christ Became Flesh* (John 1)
Monday: *Christ So Loved* (John 3)
Tuesday: *Christ Satisfies* (John 4)
Wednesday: *Christ, the Bread of Life* (John 6:1-59)
Thursday: *Christ, the Light of the World* (John 9)
Friday: *Christ, Our Shepherd* (John 10:1-39)
Saturday: *Christ Promises the Comforter* (John 14)

Memorable Quotes from Dr. Mears

"John wrote to prove that Jesus was the Christ, the promised Messiah (for the Jews), and the Son of God (for the Gentiles), and to lead believers into a life of divine friendship with Him. The Key word is 'believe.' We find this word ninety-eight times in the book."

"Sometimes the way to better understand what a thing is, is to find out what it is not. In John 1:13, John tells us what salvation is not. 'Which were born, not of blood, nor of the will of the flesh, nor of the will of man, but of God.'"

"Discipleship is tested not by the creed you recite, not by the hymns you sing, not by the ritual you observe, but by the fact that you love one another."

Looking for Yourself in God's Love Story

1. Dr. Mears talks about the three "keys" in the Gospel of John: the *back-door key* (see John 20:31), the *side-door key* (see John 16:28) and the *front-door key* (see John 1:11-12). Which of these "keys" seems to be the closest for you to reach? Which are you the most drawn to and why?

2. John's the only biblical writer to record the intimate experience of reclining against Jesus. When's the last time you "leaned" against your Savior—trusting Him to hold you, allowing yourself to collapse in His embrace?

3. John is described as both a "son of Thunder" and "the disciple Jesus loved." What do you think those titles mean, and do you think they are *complementary* or *contradictory*?

Movie Clip Moment

In the classic film *To Kill a Mockingbird* (based on Harper Lee's best-selling book), Gregory Peck plays an honorable attorney (named Atticus Finch) who fights for justice in a small-minded Southern town. It's an incredible story about integrity, ugly wounds caused by racial prejudice and the prevailing dignity of the human spirit. In much the same way that Jesus was an enigma to many, hated by some and worshiped by a few, Atticus is portrayed as a complex man who was viewed as a gruff disciplinarian by his children, heralded as a hero by the African Americans in town and seen as a traitorous villain by some of the white townspeople. There's a climactic courtroom scene toward the end of the movie—which takes place right after the unfair verdict is declared—that is an arresting depiction of *respect*. It's a sober example of the kind of esteem we're called to give God the Father. He is not our *copilot*. He is not our *buddy*. He is the King of kings and Lord of lords, who stoops down to be in relationship with us!

You Say Potato, I Say Patattah

I've had the incredible privilege of going to amazing foreign places like Africa and El Salvador on mission trips. And I've also had the frustrating experience of not being able to speak the language of the particular country I was visiting! Of course, I attempted to get over the language barrier with dramatic physical gestures, but sometimes no matter how hard I wiggle, people just can't understand what I'm trying to say. (Like the day I flapped my arms like wings but a waiter in Nairobi still served me barbequed Zebra instead of baked chicken!)

The book of Acts, which chronicles lots of exciting first-century mission trips, also underscores the importance of using relevant language in whatever corner of the world God plops us in. For example, in chapter 13 we find the apostle Paul in a stuffy setting surrounded by very religious Israelites, so he uses words that reveal his impressive grasp of Old Testament history, thereby earning those Jewish leaders' respect and creating a real base for relationship.

When Paul's hanging out with some wild and crazy guys in Athens, however (see Acts 17), he knows they'd be put off if he starts reciting Scripture–the freethinking, philosophizing Greeks were less than impressed with the Jewish emphasis on rules and regulations. So flexible Paul recites from a poem originally dedicated to Zeus, thereby revealing his comprehension of and respect for their culture! Once again, he builds a bridge for friendship with dissimilar folks, in the hopes of ultimately sharing the gospel.

Throughout the New Testament, Paul displays his mastery of *relevant communication*: of using language and stories to connect with people who do not yet share His faith in Jesus Christ.

What about you? Do your words invite unbelievers to move closer or do they cause people to walk away from you?

What's the *Story* of This Particular Book?

Acts is essentially "chapter 2" of Luke's Gospel account. The good doctor Luke wrote both books (see Acts 1:1-2): The first detailed the person and works of the Messiah, Jesus Christ, with this follow-up detailing how Christ's message was spreading throughout the ancient world like wildfire, even in the face of terrible persecution. This first-century disciple's diary also includes an account of the spectacular Damascus Road conversion of *Saul*—the haughty guy who hated Christians—to *Paul*—the humble apostle who wrote over two-thirds of the New Testament (and whose missionary journeys make up the bulk of the book of Acts)!

Henrietta's Highlights on Acts

Her Synopsis
Acts Portrays Jesus Christ, the Living Lord

Her Suggested Bible Readings

Sunday:	*First Church in Jerusalem* (Acts 1–4)
Monday:	*Witnessing in Jerusalem* (Acts 5:1–8:3)
Tuesday:	*Witnessing in Judea and Samaria* (Acts 8:4–12)
Wednesday:	*Paul Establishes the Churches* (First Tour: Acts 13:1–15:35)
Thursday:	*Paul Revisits the Churches* (Second Tour: Acts 15:36–18:21)
Friday:	*Paul Encourages the Churches* (Third Tour: Acts 18:22–25:9)
Saturday:	*Paul Sent to Rome* (Acts 25:10–28)

Memorable Quotes from Dr. Mears

"The Gospels set forth what Christ began to do. Acts shows what He continued to do by the Holy Spirit, through His disciples."

"Acts is not a record of the acts of the apostles, as no extensive accounts are given of any apostles except Peter and Paul. It records the acts of the Holy Spirit through the apostles. His name is mentioned about seventy times. Look for some work of the Holy Spirit in every chapter of this book."

Looking for Yourself in God's Love Story

1. Read Acts chapter 3. The lame beggar got infinitely more than he hoped for when he asked Peter and John for spare change! When has God's more-than-you-asked-for generosity made you want to leap for joy like this guy does?

2. Read Acts 4:23-31. This exultation—voiced by the Early Christian community when John and Peter come home after confronting the Jewish council with the gospel—is commonly called the Believer's Prayer. While its tone is jubilant, it also clearly communicates "who" killed Jesus. Describe the sober truth this passage reveals about the role God played in the crucifixion.

Movie Clip Moment

A recent release called *Babel* (2006), starring Cate Blanchett and Brad Pitt, is a fabulous film about miscommunication and how simple misunderstandings in language can have serious consequences. The film's mature themes aren't appropriate for young viewers, but I think there are several great clips for use in adult Sunday School classes or Bible studies that illustrate how important clear and authentic communication is when connecting with other people—especially when God gives us the opportunity to share with unbelievers the Living Hope that lies within us! This movie is a powerful reminder to pay attention to what rolls off our tongues. (For example, how many times have you winced when you've heard a well-intentioned Christian use "churchy" words in a fake, chipper voice around people who don't know Jesus?)

Righteousness for Ragamuffins

I think caffeine is one of God's most beneficent creations, and I think talking with friends while drinking a caffeinated beverage—preferably with two shots of espresso, skim milk and whipped cream—is even better. Add theological dialogue to the mix and you've got a beautiful experience! Suffice it to say, chatting about Jesus at the neighborhood java joint is one of my favorite activities.

It was in such a setting that I had a big "aha" moment recently. A friend and I were talking about the fantastical elements of the gospel: *The Creator of the universe condescends to the finitude of a human body, lives a perfect life without the slightest stumble in heart or motive, and then submits to a politically motivated—but divinely ordained—murder so as to redeem humanity.* Without our God-imbued faith, we'd find Star Trek plots more plausible!

My smart but spacey friend paused at one point in our weighty discussion and enthused in a strong Southern twang, "You know, I think the gospel is kind of like the Cinderella story. Christians are like Cinderella and Jesus is like the Prince."

I didn't roll my eyes and retort, "That's really dumb and doctrinally ludicrous!" But I wanted to—the comparison of God's divine love story with that of a fairy tale really rubbed me the wrong way.

After mulling it over for a while, I realized the reason I had such a strong aversion to the analogy was because Cinderella *deserved* the prince. If you've read the book or watched the DVD, you probably remember that Cinderella was beautiful. Drop-dead gorgeous. She was also a friend of animals (remember the mice?) and had an admirable work ethic. Plus, she was horribly mistreated by her Jerry Springer episode of a family. So when the slipper fits and the prince confesses his crush, most of us sigh dreamily, grateful for the happy ending—glad the good girl ends up with the good guy.

That is so *not* the gospel.

In *God's story*, the prince falls head over heels in love with the ugly stepsister—the one with moles on her face, frizzy hair, a whiney personality and elastic-waist pants. She isn't pretty, inside or out. It's a wonder the bouncers let her into the prince's party in the first place. The whole ballroom lets out a collective gasp when the handsome prince strides across the floor and asks her to dance. His choice in partners doesn't make sense. She doesn't *deserve* His affection, or anyone else's for that matter.

Then something amazing happens: As she's enveloped in the prince's adoring embrace, the stepsister *becomes* beautiful.

That's the gospel—it's infinitely better than anything Disney or Hollywood could produce! And that's the theme of Romans—a book some say is the "guts" of the gospel, the essence of God's divine love story.

What's the *Story* of This Particular Book?

The apostle Paul hears through the grapevine that some Christians in Rome are beginning to believe a heretical doctrine known as *antinomianism,* which basically means they were perverting the promise of God's redemption into a license to practice immorality. Their distorted logic goes something like this: "Since our sins are covered by the blood of Christ and we're already forgiven, let's party!" Because Paul can't get there right away to rectify the problem in person, he sits down and writes this letter, clarifying the gospel to those confused first-century believers. The result—this book called Romans—is a deeply theological and comprehensive explanation of God's amazing grace!

Henrietta's Highlights on Romans

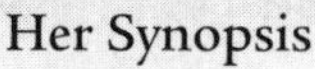

Her Synopsis

Romans Portrays Jesus Christ, Our Righteousness

Her Suggested Bible Readings

Sunday: *What We Are by Nature* (Romans 1:1–3:20)
Monday: *How to Become a Christian* (Romans 3:21–5)
Tuesday: *How to Live a Christian Life* (Romans 6)
Wednesday: *A Struggle* (Romans 7)
Thursday: *The Life of Victory* (Romans 8)
Friday: *The Jews Set Aside* (Romans 9:30–11:12)
Saturday: *The Christian's Service* (Romans 12)

Memorable Quotes from Dr. Mears

"You will find the stream of sin and the river of salvation running along together . . . Paul shows sin in all its squalor and salvation in all its splendor."

"A murderer may stand at the bottom of a mine and you on the highest peak of the highest mountain, but you are as little able to touch the stars as he. You cannot attain the righteousness that God demands, no matter how far you climb."

"The first part of Romans is what God did for us. The last part of Romans is what we may do for God."

Looking for Yourself in God's Love Story

1. Read Romans 3:22-24. What three adjectives come to mind when you consider how this passage impacts you personally?

2. What single word would you use to synopsize the first half of Romans, the *What God Did for Us* part (chapters 1 to 5)? And what word would you use to sum up the second half of Romans (chapters 6 to 12), the *What We May Do for God* part?

3. Do you find that the first or the second half of Romans resonates more with you? Explain why.

4. Read Romans 8:31-39. How have you tangibly experienced God's faithfulness?

Movie Clip Moment

In the movie *Les Miserables* (based on the book and Broadway musical by the same title), Jean Valjean is a convict who's just been released after serving 19 years in prison—for stealing food to feed his family—when he steals again, this time from the priest who was the only person to offer him food and shelter. In the scene in which the police bring Jean Valjean back to the priest to confirm the crime, the priest's startling response epitomizes grace–*unmerited favor*. This film has wonderful references to God's mercy and stirring parallels to the gospel–just make sure to stock up on Kleenex before renting it!

Pardon Me, But Your Imperfection Is Showing

You know how some people choose theme verses for their lives and they typically choose "pretty" verses or profound passages in Scripture, which vividly declare their love for God or maybe celebrate God's love for them? Well, if I had a theme verse, I'd probably choose the part of Paul's letter to the church at Corinth in which he says that God deliberately chooses things the world considers foolish and weak in order to shame those who think they're really something. The bottom line (no pun intended) is that I'm the poster child for imperfection—every time I turn around, my flaws are revealed with a flourish!

One of my more colorful displays of foolishness happened when I was working at Focus on the Family in Colorado Springs. I got to work there for six years and thoroughly enjoyed the experience, so it was bittersweet when I decided to take a job in Nashville. I spent the last several weeks at Focus connecting with as many people as possible. One afternoon, when I was walking back toward my office from the restroom, I ran into a gentleman who worked in the department across from mine. I was really glad to see him, because we both traveled a lot and I wasn't sure I'd actually get to say goodbye face to face. We stood there in the hallway for a while—talking about God's sovereignty and how He orders our steps—and I found myself thinking how fortunate I was to have the opportunity to work with people like him.

It was a wonderful conversation, except for one little detail: The whole time we were talking this guy wouldn't look directly at me. And you know how you expect someone to look you in the eye when you're having a one-on-one conversation, especially if the conversation is personal? I kept trying to insert myself into his line of vision—tried to maneuver myself so that he'd *have* to look at me—but he still just kept staring away from me. I thought, *Oh, well . . . he's so smart; he's probably just preoccupied with some Greek passage in John's Gospel.*

When we finished our conversation a few minutes later, he turned and walked briskly back toward his office. But when I turned to walk toward mine, I felt a little draft, glanced down and was horrified to see that I'd accidentally tucked my skirt into my underwear when I was in the restroom! To make matters worse, I was wearing thigh highs. Obviously, my modest male friend had been staring off at the horizon while we contemplated the sovereign mercies of God because he was absolutely traumatized by the sight of me in my near-natural state!

I don't know if you've ever had an indecent-exposure experience like mine, but I'm sure you have a few of your own embarrassing stories, moments when your weakness was more apparent that your winsomeness. The good news of the gospel that Paul reiterates in this book is that God is well aware of our blemishes. He's not surprised by our shortcomings. Miraculously, He cherishes us anyway.

What's the *Story* of This Particular Book?

Paul established this "church plant" in Corinth on his second missionary journey (see Acts 18). And while there were some very gifted people in this young congregation, they still got off to a pretty rocky start—partly because they were plotted right in the middle of a lascivious Greek society, so carnal temptations were everywhere (think Las Vegas), and partly because there were a lot of stinkers in this body of believers and gossip and infighting were a regular occurrence. Therefore, Paul pens a letter to these precious yet immature new believers, basically telling them to grow up and learn to get along!

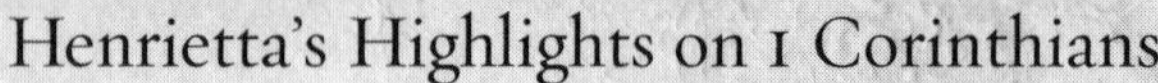

Henrietta's Highlights on 1 Corinthians

Her Synopsis
First Corinthians Portrays Jesus Christ, Our Lord

Her Suggested Bible Readings
Sunday: *Division in the Church* (1 Corinthians 1:10-31)
Monday: *Human Wisdom* (1 Corinthians 2)
Tuesday: *Worldliness in the Church* (1 Corinthians 3)
Wednesday: *Immorality in the Church* (1 Corinthians 5)
Thursday: *The Lord's Supper* (1 Corinthians 11)
Friday: *Hymn of Love* (1 Corinthians 13)
Saturday: *The Resurrection* (1 Corinthians 15)

Memorable Quotes from Dr. Mears
"It was all right for the church to be in Corinth, but it was fatal when Corinth got into the church. It is a glorious sight to see a ship launched into the sea, but it is a tragic sight when the sea gets into the ship."

"Jesus Christ is the only cure for division (1 Corinthians 1:13). Every eye, every heart, every spirit must be turned to one object–Jesus Christ, our personal Savior."

"Paul did not preach Christ the conqueror or Christ the philosopher, but Christ crucified, Christ the humble."

"God used to have a temple for His people; now He has a people for a temple."

Looking for Yourself in God's Love Story

1. When you do something really foolish or embarrassing, do you imagine God grinning or grimacing?

2. Read 1 Corinthians 8–10. In light of what Paul teaches about exercising Christian liberty, what quality do

you think should always coexist with spiritual freedom? When do you think it's a good idea to intentionally *limit your liberty*?

3. First Corinthians 13 is probably the most well-known biblical passage about love—how would you summarize this chapter in one sentence? What's your favorite verse in this inspirational section and why?

Movie Clip Moment

In the 1998 comedy *Waking Ned Devine,* an Irish village behaves much like the community of Corinthian Christians. The citizens of Tullymore are a bumbling, stumbling, sometimes deceitful and greedy crew—and you'll probably find someone in the cast who closely resembles you! The heartwarming part of this story is that despite dissention, people who care about each other ultimately come together in a dysfunctional family kind of way—which reminds me of a healthy church: It's a place full of broken people who tend to bump up against each other too hard, but who will ultimately huddle together for comfort when the cold winds of hardship blow.

It's Really *Not* "All About Me"

I recently listened to a 20-year-old give her testimony to a group of high school girls, and I got tickled because she was so emotive. Her highs and lows were recited with the flare of an Academy Award-winning actress. A recent breakup with her boyfriend was recounted with all the melodrama of Juliet's farewell to Romeo. Listening to her tell her story was like watching a movie in an IMAX theater—you know, those fancy theaters with digital surround-sound systems and huge screens that depict three-dimensional, larger-than-life images?

Later that night I was smiling to myself and thinking how narcissistic college co-eds can be, when I realized that watching her was like looking in a mirror. Maturity has tempered my melodrama a bit so that I don't talk about myself quite as loudly or colorfully as she did. However, I'm still a card-carrying member of egocentric cinema. Some days I'm a walking, talking *me*-MAX theater, proudly screening a movie with myself in the starring role. Thankfully, God is quick and gracious to remind me that the world does not revolve around me.

Soon after that experience, I had lunch with the president of a Christian publishing company, and I was feeling a little smug because it's not every day one gets to meet with a head honcho in the publishing world. We were having a great conversation when he said, "Kim, I'd like to get your address for my Palm Pilot." I thought, *Surely he didn't just call me Kim. Maybe he just pronounces "Lisa" weird.* But I could read the writing in his notebook, and he'd definitely written "K-I-M" in big, black letters. Here I was, thinking I was on the cusp of literary greatness, and my publisher didn't even know my name! It was a not-so-subtle reminder from the Holy Spirit that my ego was showing.

A. W. Tozer comments on our self-involvement in his book *The Pursuit of God*:

> Within the human heart things have taken over. Men have now by nature no peace within their hearts, for God is crowned there no longer, but there in the moral dusk,

> stubborn and aggressive usurpers fight among themselves for the first place on the throne.[4]

Self-centered cinema is one of the most aggressive usurpers of peace and unity in the Body of Christ. When loving God and others takes a back seat to the consuming daily drama of our lives, dissention will most definitely take root among us—when we're preoccupied with playing the lead, we take our eyes off Jesus. Therefore, as His beloved daughters, we've been called to close our *me*-MAX theaters, acknowledging and practicing the simple biblical truth that the world doesn't revolve around us.

What's the *Story* of This Particular Book?

Paul returned to this problematic congregation when he found out more trouble had risen to the surface. Someone (probably a false prophet) was slandering the apostle Paul's reputation so as to discredit the gospel. The visit didn't go as planned because these Corinthian stinkers weren't very receptive to their founder's warning. Like me on that literary date, their ego was getting in the way! So Paul leaves and travels back to his ministry headquarters in Ephesus, no doubt with a heavy heart—when he gets home, he takes out a pen and writes this letter—sometimes referred to as the "stern" letter—to convince the Corinthians of their need to repent.

Henrietta's Highlights on 2 Corinthians

Her Synopsis
Second Corinthians Portrays Jesus Christ, Our Sufficiency

Her Suggested Bible Readings

Sunday: *Christ Our Comfort* (2 Corinthians 1–2)
Monday: *Living Epistles* (2 Corinthians 3–4)
Tuesday: *Ambassadors for Christ* (2 Corinthians 5–6)
Wednesday: *The Heart of Paul* (2 Corinthians 7:1–8:15)
Thursday: *Christian Giving* (2 Corinthians 8:16–9)
Friday: *Paul's Apostleship* (2 Corinthians 10–11)
Saturday: *God's Strength* (2 Corinthians 12–13)

Memorable Quotes from Dr. Mears

"Paul finds his comfort through all his troubles in the fact of the resurrection that Christ promised. He lived under the inspiration of the fact that one day he was to have a changed, glorified body."

"We all have a tendency to take a wrong standard for measuring character. We compare ourselves among ourselves. We conclude we are as good as the average. But average Christians are not what the Bible requires."

"Do not depend on a mere profession of religion. Do not rely on church membership. Joining the church saves no one. Joining Christ saves us. Examine your standing."

Looking for Yourself in God's Love Story

1. Read 2 Corinthians 4:7-18. In light of how Paul had been slandered and publicly humiliated, what's significant about his "jars of clay" metaphor?

2. Read 2 Corinthians 9:7-9. Do you feel secretly *guilty* about how much—or how little—you give God financially, or do you feel *glad*?

3. Read 2 Corinthians 10:5. I have a guy friend who, inspired by this verse, says that we should grab our thoughts and "frisk them"—much like a policeman will throw a criminal suspect up against a wall and pat him down! What metaphor (perhaps a more feminine one!) would you use to illustrate Paul's point here?

Movie Clip Moment

Robert Duvall portrays "Sonny," a Pentecostal preacher—and at times, a fantastically *false* prophet—in the 1997 drama *The Apostle.* Much like the movie *Saved!* (see the Gospel of Mark), the storyline paints a very unflattering—albeit sometimes accurate—portrait of Christians. Furthermore, the flaws in this fictional community of faith bring to mind the deception Paul confronted in Corinth. The action takes place in the rural South and the scenery is a beautiful contrast to Sonny's ugly megalomania. Several other well-known actors (Farrah Fawcett, Billy Bob Thornton and Miranda Richardson) add to the quality of this film. Watching it will make you wonder why some believers build up the Body of Christ and others seem determined to tear it down, brick by brick. And it might just move you to repent!

Busy Hands and Cold Hearts

Several years ago, one of my friends complained to her husband that she wished they could spend just a little more quality time together. She was busy with their new baby and he was busy starting a new law practice, so between diapers and depositions they'd begun to behave like roommates instead of a happily married couple.

Her husband is a pretty pragmatic guy, so after listening to her sincere lament, he asked her *exactly* what she meant by "more quality time." She explained that while she expected their lives to be different with children and his burgeoning career, and she understood that they'd probably never have the amount of private time they used to enjoy as newlyweds, she just wished that every once in a while they could spend 20 minutes in the evening just sitting on the porch swing and talking.

The very next evening, she was pleasantly surprised when he suggested that they go sit out on the swing after they'd washed the dinner dishes and put the baby to bed. It was a beautiful night and as they sat there chatting, she thought to herself, *This is so great! I feel just as close to him as I did on our honeymoon!* But then—right in the middle of her romantic nostalgia—her husband lifted his arm from around her shoulders, looked at his watch and said, "Okay, it's been 20 minutes. Are we alright now?"

He'd fulfilled his obligation. He'd crossed his martial *T*s and dotted his relational *I*s, but his soul just wasn't in it. He had responded to the literal words of her request rather that the cry of her heart . . . which basically describes how the Galatians were learning to respond to their Creator. Through the influence of false teachers, they were starting to focus on being religious instead of being in relationship with Jesus. They were trying to follow God's rules and regulations but their hearts were growing cold and leaking hope.

What's the *Story* of This Particular Book?

Paul preached this sermon to the easily-led-astray Galatians so as to clarify the distorted doctrine they'd adopted because of persuasive "Judaizers" (Jewish "Christians" who were trying to tack the regulations of the Old Testament–like circumcision–onto the free gift of grace). The gist of his message is that legalism doesn't have anything to do with loving God, and he explains that salvation equals trusting-in-Jesus-plus-nothing-else!

Henrietta's Highlights on Galatians

Her Synopsis
Galatians Portrays Jesus Christ, Our Liberty

Her Suggested Bible Readings
Sunday: *Only One Gospel* (Galatians 1)
Monday: *Justified by Faith* (Galatians 2)
Tuesday: *The Law Points to Christ* (Galatians 3)
Wednesday: *Law and Grace* (Galatians 4)
Thursday: *Stand Fast in Christian Liberty* (Galatians 5:1-16)
Friday: *Flesh Versus Spirit* (Galatians 5:17-26)
Saturday: *Sowing and Reaping* (Galatians 6)

Memorable Quotes from Dr. Mears
"False teachers had begun to 'bewitch' the people by telling them they must keep all kinds of ceremonies. Paul wanted them to know that nothing, no fetishes or works or ceremonies could bring them to Christ. Salvation comes by believing in Christ–nothing else."

"A religion without the cross is not Christ's religion. Christ did not come merely to blaze a trail through a tangled forest or to set us an example of true living. He came to be a Savior."

Looking for Yourself in God's Love Story

1. Did you grow up in a church that emphasized legalism or were your childhood spiritual lessons more "loose"?

2. In your own words, how would you define "Christian liberty"?

3. What would you say is the key difference between having religion and having peace with God?

Movie Clip Moment

Chocolat is a clever film from 2000 with a notable cast that includes Juliette Binoche, Alfred Molina, Judi Dench, Lena Olin and Johnny Depp. The storyline is about a woman—the single mother of a young daughter—who opens a chocolate shop in a moralistic French village during Lent. The rigid townspeople opposed to her sweet confections will remind you of the rigid New Testament legalists who were opposed to the sweet freedom found at the foot of the cross. The best clip takes place near the end of the movie when Juliette and Johnny teach the town a lesson about true compassion.

Consider What's Coming Out of Your Mouth

Not too long ago I came home from work—tired and irritated after a long, hard day—to find that my dog had "decorated" the new carpeting. I hadn't chosen this particular dog—I had inherited her from a friend who asked me to keep her while he found a permanent home for her. Long story short, she'd been at my house for three years (if you read the devotion in Malachi, you already know the final chapter of her particular story). She wasn't even my type: She weighed 11 pounds and I like big dogs; she was very sassy and I like sweet dogs; her name was Reba (her prior owner is a Nashville songwriter) and I don't really like country music. But she had kind of grown on me, and I thought that at least her diminutive size meant she wouldn't make much of a mess in the house. Surprise.

I was so mad when I walked into the den and found her "present" on the brand-new cream-colored Berber. The rest of the house has hardwood floors or tile *and* she had a doggie-door to go outside, so her "deed" was defiant! She looked up from her bed with a smirk and all but dared me to discipline her. I lost my cool, took two quick strides across the room, grabbed Reba by the scruff of the neck, slung open the side door and threw her (ever so gently) outside, yelling about what a bad dog she was the whole time! I finished with a flourish, while she yelped in exaggerated terror.

It was at that very moment I heard my neighbor, a lovely woman named Vicky, call for her four-year-old, Connor, to come inside. Our houses are only about 30 feet apart, separated by a small privacy fence, so she no doubt heard my temper tantrum loud and clear. She obviously wanted to remove her innocent child from earshot of her crazy, dog-abusing neighbor! My embarrassing outburst reminded me of something Paul said in Ephesians: "Do not let any unwholesome talk come out of your mouths, but only what is helpful for building others up according to their needs, that it may benefit those who listen" (Ephesians 4:29).

If you're like most women, your mouth gets you in trouble every now and then. Sometimes our language is less than wholesome and falls well below favorable. A good question for us to ask ourselves in light of these verses is: *Do my words benefit others and serve as a bridge for the gospel?* Or—like my "terrier tirade"—*Do my words act as barbs, creating barriers between myself and others?*

Has your tongue been tempered by God's love?

What's the *Story* of This Particular Book?

Mission-minded Paul had planted this church in Ephesus (see Acts 19), and the believers there had started off with a big gospel bang. Pastor Paul wants to make sure they stay on track so he sends this letter, which reads like a "good doctrine instruction manual" to keep them on the straight and narrow. One of the most practical biblical teachings about Christian preparedness—about facing the difficulties of the day head-on (also a perennial favorite in Vacation Bible Schools)—is the "armor of God" admonition in chapter 6.

Henrietta's Highlights on Ephesians

Her Synopsis
Ephesians Portrays Jesus Christ, Our All in All

Her Suggested Bible Readings

Sunday: *The Believer's Position* (Ephesians 1)
Monday: *Saved by Grace* (Ephesians 2)
Tuesday: *A Mystery Revealed* (Ephesians 3)
Wednesday: *A Christian's Walk* (Ephesians 4)
Thursday: *Following Christ* (Ephesians 5:1-20)
Friday: *Living with Others* (Ephesians 5:21–6:9)
Saturday: *Christian Warfare* (Ephesians 6:10-24)

Memorable Quotes from Dr. Mears

"In this Epistle, we enter the holy of holies in Paul's writing."

"When God puts upon us His jewels of grace, He seals us by His Spirit (Ephesians 4:30). It is like a young man putting a diamond upon the engagement finger of one whom he has promised to marry."

"Now we stand in a room hung with the whole armor of God. The armor is His, not ours! But He tells us to put it on. We must put on the whole of it if we will be safe. The armor is not for a museum where we can go and look over its strength, but it is for the battlefield. Polished armor hanging up in the hall of our creed will not save us in the day of battle."

"Stand, Christian, in the victory of Christ wrought on Calvary. But you notice there is no armor for the back. The Christian is never supposed to run from enemies, but fight the good fight of faith, praying always!"

Looking for Yourself in God's Love Story

1. Read Ephesians 2:10. The word "workmanship" comes from the Greek word *poiema*, which means a "poem," or "masterpiece." So you're a "work of art" in God's estimation! What poem or painting comes to mind when you think about Him?

2. Read Ephesians 2:19-22. This passage refers to the unity that should be evident among Christians, regardless of their nationality, language or color. Where and when have you experienced *real community* with other believers? Would you describe your church as a place of unity? Why or why not?

3. Read Ephesians 6:10-24. Which piece of armor do you find the most difficult to wear? Explain why.

Movie Clip Moment

There's a dramatic scene in *Braveheart* in which Mel Gibson (playing the brave Scotsman William Wallace) rides his horse up and down the front line so as to motivate his men. Although they're facing a much larger English army, you can sense the courage sparking in the Scotsmen. They just can't wait to attack the seemingly wimpy, well-dressed Brits! It's one of the most stirring pre-fight scenes ever captured on film and is a great inspirational tool to keep in mind as we contemplate the "armor of God" passage. Watching this clip always makes me want to strap on that divine breastplate as fast as I can and go charge some unholy hill!

The Fuel of Good Friendship

I'm not typically a fan of forwarded emails. Frankly, I delete pretty much anything that's "forwarded" without so much as a glance. But a funny friend sent this essay (I haven't been able to find out who the original author was), and I found it so hilarious that I thought I'd "forward" it to y'all . . . because sometimes sharing a belly laugh with girlfriends is exactly the kind of fuel we need to keep going in this sometimes difficult walk of faith.

Swimsuit Agony

When I was a child in the 1960s, the bathing suit for the womanly figure was boned, trussed and reinforced, not so much sewn as engineered. They were built to hold back and uplift and they did a good job.

Today's stretch fabrics are designed for the prepubescent girl with a figure carved from a potato chip. The curvaceous woman has a choice: She can either go to the maternity department and try on a floral suit with a skirt made for a hippopotamus who escaped from Disney's Fantasia, or she can do her best to make a sensible choice from a designer range of florescent rubber bands.

What choice did I have? I wandered around, made my sensible choice and entered the chamber of horrors known as the fitting room.

I believe the Lycra used in bathing costumes was developed by NASA to launch small rockets from a slingshot. The good news is that if you manage to maneuver yourself into one, you are protected from shark attacks—any shark taking a swipe would immediately suffer whiplash.

I fought my way into the bathing suit, and as I twanged the shoulder strap in place, I gasped in horror: My boobs had disappeared! Eventually I found one boob cowering under my left armpit, but it took a while to find the other.

At last I located it, flattened beside my seventh rib.

I realigned my assets and lurched toward the mirror to take a full-view assessment. The suit fit all right, but only those bits of me willing to stay inside it. The rest of me oozed out from top, bottom and sides. As I tried to work out where all those extra chunks had come from, the tiny sales girl popped her head through the curtain. "Oh, there you are!" she said, admiring the bathing suit. I asked what else she had to show me.

I tried on a cream crinkled one that made me look like a lump of masking tape and a floral two-piece which gave me the appearance of an oversized napkin in a serving ring. I struggled into a pair of leopard skin bathers with ragged frills and came out looking like Tarzan's Jane, pregnant with triplets and having a rough day. I tried on a black number with a midriff cutout and looked like a jellyfish in mourning. I tried on a bright pink affair with such a high-cut leg, I would've had to wax my eyebrows to wear it.

Finally I found a suit that fit: a two-piece with a shorts-style bottom and a loose, blouse-type top. It was cheap, comfortable and bulge-friendly, so I bought it. My ridiculous search had a successful outcome, I figured, but when I got home, I found a label that read, "Material might become transparent in water."

I've decided that this summer, I'll be the one in cut-off jeans and a T-shirt!

I don't know if they forwarded funny "e-pistles" in the first century or not, but I'm sure that the apostles were energized and encouraged by their close friends, because that theme is at the very heart of Philippians. This is the little book in the New Testament that is full of verses most likely to be memorized by youth group devotees!

What's the *Story* of This Particular Book?

Philippians is kind of like Paul's "Hallmark card" to the believers living in Philippi. He begins by expressing his deep gratitude for their financial and prayerful support while he was incarcerated in

Rome. Then he goes on to affirm their exemplary Christian character. It's immediately obvious by the tone of his language that Paul really loves these faraway Philippian friends! His affection prompts him to share a gentle warning in closing: He encourages them to keep their guard up, to protect the genuine relationships and all the good things happening in their midst.

Henrietta's Highlights on Philippians

Her Synopsis
Philippians Portrays Jesus Christ, Our Joy

Her Suggested Bible Readings

Sunday:	*Joy Triumphs over Suffering* (Philippians 1)
Monday:	*Joy in Christ* (Philippians 2:1-11)
Tuesday:	*Joy in Salvation* (Philippians 2:12-30)
Wednesday:	*Joy in Christ's Righteousness* (Philippians 3:1-9)
Thursday:	*Joy in Christ's Will* (Philippians 3:10-21)
Friday:	*Joy in Christ's Strength* (Philippians 4:1-7)
Saturday:	*Joy in Christ's Provision* (Philippians 4:8-23)

Memorable Quotes from Dr. Mears
"It hardly seems possible that Paul is writing from prison with chains holding him. His words seem to come from a light heart. It is evident that the soul of this great apostle is free! There is an atmosphere of joy even from prison."

"Paul tells the Philippians that the duty of all Christians is that they be joyful. A long-faced Christian is the worst advertisement against Christianity."

Looking for Yourself in God's Love Story

1. Read Philippians 1:9-11. Consider writing these verses on a card along with the names of friends and family that you're praying this blessing for.

2. Read Philippians 2:14-16. Do you know a Christian you'd describe as a "shining star" because of his or her obvious love for God and others? Do you think anyone in your circle of relationships would describe you as "shiny"?

3. Read Philippians 4:19. This promise about God's provision can become so familiar that we almost forget the miracle it declares. List some of the tangible ways God has recently met all your needs.

Movie Clip Moment

In the effort to recommend some movies that are appropriate for all ages, I'm going with the animated, will-one-day-be-called-a-classic, *Toy Story* (1995). With voice and inflection provided by the likes of Tom Hanks, Tim Allen, Jim Varney and Don Rickles, this film is thoroughly entertaining, even if you don't wear short pants anymore! You might not bust a gut laughing, but you'll at least giggle. And while tickling your funny bone, the storyline will also prick your heart as it emphasizes the value of friendship. I think this is another good flick to enjoy with the children in your life and then chat about spiritual parallels afterward.

If It Were a Snake, It Would Have Bitten You

A few weeks ago I was racing around my house because I needed to leave for a meeting, but I couldn't find my sunglasses anywhere. Which may not sound like a big deal to you, but shades are as important to me as shoes (which is saying quite a lot!) because my pupils don't dilate correctly from too many summers spent as a squinting lifeguard. Thus, without sunglasses I have a hard time driving or doing much of anything outside . . . I'm kind of like a human mole.

I looked frantically for my glasses in all of the likely places: my purse, the top of the dresser, the dining room table. Then, with the clock ticking and my frustration mounting, I started looking in weird places, like inside the refrigerator, the freezer and the washing machine. Eventually I got down on the floor to look under my bed, thinking maybe I'd accidentally kicked them beyond the dust ruffle. But I couldn't see anything because it was so dark. That's when I realized that my sunglasses had been perched on my nose the whole time!

I am often similarly surprised by scriptural truths that have been right in front of my face for years. Sometimes I'll read a story that I've been familiar with since childhood and all of the sudden, *Wham!* I'm bowled over by our Creator's kindness. Stunned by His accessibility. Wowed by His sufficiency. I think those of us who've walked with God for a season need to be careful about becoming spiritually near-sighted. We should guard against becoming oblivious to the obvious.

Have you let your familiarity with the gospel cloud your view of His glory?

What's the *Story* of This Particular Book?

An enthusiastic convert of Paul's named Epaphras planted the church in Colosse (see Colossians 1:7), and while they'd begun with a bang, running smoothly on the right theological track, they were now being brainwashed by a bunch of losers parading as deep-thinking evangelists. Epaphras kept waving the gospel right in front of his congregation's face, but they were no longer recognizing the truth. The frustrated pastor took off for Rome to ask Paul to write a literary wake-up call, and this book is the result.

Henrietta's Highlights on Colossians

Her Synopsis
Colossians Portrays Jesus Christ, Our Life

Her Suggested Bible Readings

Sunday: *Paul's Greeting and Prayer* (Colossians 1:1-14)
Monday: *Seven Superiorities of Christ* (Colossians 1:15-29)
Tuesday: *Christ Exalted* (Philippians 2:1-16)
Wednesday: *Complete in Christ* (Colossians 2:17-19)
Thursday: *Old and New Man* (Colossians 2:20–3:11)
Friday: *Christian Living* (Colossians 3:12-25)
Saturday: *Christian Graces* (Colossians 4)

Memorable Quotes from Dr. Mears

"Christ is all in all. The failure of the Colossians was at this very point, not holding fast to the Lord. The place Christ holds in any religious teaching determines whether it is true or false."

"Christianity is not a series of giving-ups; it is a new life. Children do not give up playing jacks; they outgrow it. As we come to know Christ better, we find that some things no longer interest us."

Looking for Yourself in God's Love Story

1. The behavioral guidelines for Christians in Colossians 3–4:6 are kind of like the "What Would Jesus Do" for every situation in life. Which one of Paul's directives is easy for you to follow, and which one is the most difficult for you to practice?

2. One of the basic heresies prevalent in Colosse seems to have been *Dualism*—which held that the physical world (all that we can see, feel, smell and touch) was less valuable than the spirit world we can't tangibly experience. Accordingly, Jesus would not have been as high on the "spiritual totem pole" as angels because He came to Earth in a physical body and hugged dirty lepers and stuff. They even argued that He was "less than" because of the way He loved people! How might people miss the huge errors in this teaching—people who, after all, have *bodies*? (By the way, have you gotten your hands "dirty for God" lately?)

3. Read Colossians 3:23-24. How do you think these verses relate to Eric Liddel's famous "When I run, I feel God's pleasure" line (from the movie *The Chariots of Fire*)? Are you really engaged in your daily responsibilities this season, or do you find yourself simply going through the motions?

Movie Clip Moment

Emma is the 1996 movie (starring Gwyneth Paltrow) based on Jane Austin's novel by the same name. Emma is a well-intentioned young lady who has a habit of intruding in other people's personal matters, especially their romantic matters, but she's constantly—often comically—off the mark as a matchmaker! And in spite of her preoccupation with other people's love lives, Emma is totally clueless when it comes to her own heart. There are several priceless scenes between her and the chivalrous Mr. Knightly as Emma epitomizes someone who's totally blind to the treasure that's right in front of her.

Looking Through Smudged Lenses

I used to love trail running when I lived in Colorado. One of my favorite trails was in a place called Palmer Park—it winds up about two-and-a-half miles through evergreen trees and then ends in an alpine meadow with a spectacular view of Pike's Peak. It was the place I went to gather my thoughts and commune with the Lord at the end of especially long days—basically my own personal Psalm 23 green pasture.

So I was really disappointed when I heard reports of criminal activity that was supposedly taking place in Palmer Park. Television reporters and newspaper articles gave details of violent crimes against women and said police were also looking for a man who'd exposed himself to unsuspecting hikers. They gave grim-faced warnings about not using park trails until the criminal elements were apprehended.

But on one beautiful, blue-sky fall afternoon I thought, *It's just too pretty for criminal activity today!* And I decided it was worth the risk to run my favorite trail once more. I ran in perfect solitude for a while, singing worship songs and breathing deeply the crisp mountain air. Then, right before I stepped into the alpine meadow, I stopped dead in my tracks behind a big pine tree because about 50 feet in front of me was a naked man.

I thought, *I can't believe this—I've run right into the criminal in his birthday suit!* At first I was indignant, thinking how this creep was ruining the great outdoors. But then I got scared as I realized how vulnerable I was. I hadn't seen another person since the parking lot and I wondered, *Oh, gosh, what if he sees me and starts chasing me?* My mind started racing. Filled with fear, I could only focus on two clear thoughts. One: I'd read somewhere that men who expose themselves are typically cowards. Two: I'd read somewhere else that if you came upon a wild animal in the Rockies—unless it was a bear—you should put your arms over your head and advance toward the creature while speaking in deep, guttural tones because then it'd be intimidated and probably run away.

I took a deep breath, then jumped out from behind the tree and ran toward the guy screaming and waving my arms over my head. My strategy worked, because he jumped up, obviously alarmed, and started sprinting away in the opposite direction. It was only then that I noticed his tiny blue shorts that hadn't previously been visible. He kept glancing back over his shoulder as he made his hasty retreat, seemingly terrified that I was going to chase *him*!

I had been absolutely certain that man didn't have a stitch on—but daylight was fading fast, a tree jutted into the sightline and the media had infected me with apprehension. My addled observation skills had caused me to traumatize an innocent man. He's probably still in therapy, trying to get over his phobia of screaming women in the woods!

The potential damage caused by blurry vision is infinitely worse in the spiritual arena. When we distort God's character (who He is) and our calling (who He's created us to be), our lenses are smudged and we need fresh eyes to see the truth.

What's the *Story* of This Particular Book?

The young believers in the bustling city of Thessalonica were definitely suffering from fuzzy spiritual vision. They were full of enthusiasm about their faith, but they had an immature understanding of their role as Christ's ambassadors—of what it meant to "live Christianly." They were especially unclear about the second coming of the Messiah, so their favorite evangelist, the apostle Paul, wrote this pastoral note encouraging them to *focus*!

Henrietta's Highlights on 1 Thessalonians

Her Synopsis

First Thessalonians Portrays Jesus Christ, the Coming One

Her Suggested Bible Readings

Sunday: *Christ's Coming an Inspiration to Young Christians* (1 Thessalonians 1)

Monday: *Christ's Coming an Encouragement to the Faithful* (1 Thessalonians 2)

Tuesday: *Christ's Coming an Incentive to Love Among Christians* (1 Thessalonians 3:1–4:12)

Wednesday: *Christ's Coming a Comfort to the Bereaved* (1 Thessalonians 4:13-18)

Thursday: *Christ's Coming a Challenge to Holy Living* (1 Thessalonians 5)

Friday: *Christ's Sudden Coming* (Matthew 24:1-27)

Saturday: *Tribulation Days* (Matthew 24:29-51)

Memorable Quotes from Dr. Mears

"The second coming of the Lord Jesus Christ is the truth Paul is presenting in these two letters to the Thessalonians, and it would be missing the mark not to recognize it."

"This is an intimate Epistle. The letter is a heart-to-heart talk."

"A Christian's walk is a Christian's life . . . Our walk and our talk should be twins going along on the same trail."

Looking for Yourself in God's Love Story

1. Read 1 Thessalonians 2:3-7. The gist of Paul's message here is to dance for God's pleasure, not before the altar of human approval. What person's approval—or lack thereof—are you most affected by?

2. Read 1 Thessalonians 2:8. Have you been more encouraged in your faith by Christian *relationships* or Christian *activities*?

Movie Clip Moment

I'm not a big golf fan, so I'm usually not fond of golf films, but *The Legend of Baggar Vance* is about much more than maneuvering a tiny, dimpled ball into an almost-as-tiny cup. The heart of this movie is about redemption. The plot involves a mysterious caddy named Baggar (played convincingly by Will Smith) and a gifted but haunted athlete named Rannulph Junuh (played by Matt Damon). The story unfolds slowly (like most Robert Redford projects), but it packs a powerful lesson about learning to see clearly again after clouds have dimmed your soul for far too long. And the warm, mentoring relationship between Will and Matt just might remind you a little bit of Paul and the Thessalonians!

Pursuing with Passion

My dogs—Jack Russell terriers named Harley and Dot—have sweet dispositions and I think they're smart. They usually come when I call them, and they can both sit and stay on command, but I've never tried to teach them any truly fancy pet tricks, like how to play dead, prance around in a tutu or play a musical instrument. Thus, I wasn't sure what they were actually capable of . . . until last week, when my dog's abilities amazed me!

I was working in the yard and I had both of them tethered to a yard stake so that they could run *around* but not run *away* (they're absolutely enamored with the hundreds of acres of federal land preserve—crammed full of rabbits and other creatures to chase—behind my house). But then I got distracted talking to a workman for a minute, and when I looked up, the dogs had vanished.

Somehow they'd pulled the stake out of the ground and taken off with it and the 40-foot lead that had been clipped to their collars. I wasn't too worried at first because they had run off in the woods before and always come back within a few hours, usually covered with mud and briars and ticks, but otherwise safe and sound. Yet when I realized they were probably still dragging the stake and the long wire lead, I thought about how they could get tangled up and get hurt. So I jumped in my car and went searching all their usual haunts. After that fruitless search, I pulled on hiking boots and tromped through the woods calling their names over and over again. Harley and Dot had disappeared.

So I went back to gardening, albeit anxious and distracted. I stopped every few minutes to call them and listen for barking. About an hour later I was rewarded with a weak bark, and Harley came loping down the backyard hill with his tongue hanging out. But Dottie wasn't with him, and he wouldn't stop pacing or whining even after I gave him a treat.

Suddenly I had an idea.

I clipped Harley back to his leash and said, "Find Dottie, Harley!" While I didn't know if he understood the command, he took off running like he did—as I huffed and puffed behind, trying desperately to keep up. Much to my surprise, he galloped a direct path up though the woods, straight to his sister, Dottie, who was trapped wide-eyed in the underbrush with the blue lead wrapped around her little furry neck. If she'd been left there alone much longer, she probably would have choked to death. I was so thankful for Harley's hidden bloodhound gifts that I couldn't stop petting him. And of course, both dogs got giant welcome-home bones!

Afterward I found myself wondering, *What if I were as passionate in pursuing a more intimate relationship with Jesus as Harley was about tracking Dottie?*

What's the *Story* of This Particular Book?

The bottom line is that many in the church at Thessalonica were lazy! While the congregation had grown in numbers, they weren't growing in spiritual maturity. Instead of passionately pursuing a closer walk with Christ, they were crashed out on the couch eating donuts and watching reruns. Their philosophy was basically this: *Since Jesus is coming back anyway, we might as well relax until He returns to carry us off to heaven!* So Paul pulls out his trusty pen and fires off another pastoral letter to clarify their faulty doctrine and encourage them to turn off the TV and start a Bible study in Starbucks—or something along those lines.

Henrietta's Highlights on 2 Thessalonians

Her Synopsis

Second Thessalonians Portrays Jesus Christ, Our Returning Lord

Her Suggested Bible Readings

Sunday: *Paul's Salutations* (Ephesians 1:1-2; Philippians 1:1-4; Colossians 1:1-3; 1 Thessalonians 1:1-3; 2 Thessalonians 1:1-4)

Monday: *Christ's Coming Our Comfort* (2 Thessalonians 1:5-12)

Tuesday: *Events Preceding Christ's Coming* (2 Thessalonians 2:1-12)

Wednesday: *An Appeal to Sound Doctrine* (2 Thessalonians 2:13-17)

Thursday: *The Close of the Age* (Matthew 24:13-31)
Friday: *Warnings to the Wicked Concerning His Coming* (Matthew 24:30-31; Mark 8:38; 2 Thessalonians 1:7-8; Jude 14-15; Revelation 1:7)
Saturday: *Consistent Christian Conduct* (2 Thessalonians 3)

Memorable Quotes from Dr. Mears

"The hope of Christ's coming stimulates without exciting; sobers without depressing. It is a balancing doctrine."

"Any view of Christianity that makes a man neglect working for his livelihood is not of God."

Looking for Yourself in God's Love Story

Read 2 Thessalonians 3:1-15, 1 Corinthians 5:1-13 and Galatians 6:1-5. The word "accountability" can mean vastly different things to different people; based on these passages, how would you describe God's view of Christian accountability?

Movie Clip Moment

One of the best movies clips of all times (in my very biased opinion!) comes from the movie *Chariots of Fire*. Midway through this movie–which is based on the true story of Eric Liddell, a devout Christian and 1924 Olympic champion–Eric has a confrontation with his oh-so-serious sister. She's concerned about how his running might affect his call as a missionary. But his reply silences her apprehension and personifies holy passion. I've shown this inspirational scene many times in Bible studies through the years and always ask the question, "What's your 'I feel God's pleasure' activity?" afterward. It's a great catalyst for conversation regarding what the passionate pursuit of what God's delight can/should look like.

Just Breathe

The biblical duo of Mary and Martha (see Luke 10:38-42) reminds me a lot of another juxtaposed pair named Oscar and Felix. Remember them? They were the main characters on that '70s show *The Odd Couple*. Felix was high strung and persnickety with perhaps a touch of OCD, while Oscar was a lovable—albeit grumpy—slob. Of course this pop-culture comparison isn't a perfect theological metaphor, because though Martha does come across as fussy, Scripture doesn't say Mary was slovenly! It simply reveals that she wasn't defined by *doing*. "She had a sister called Mary, who sat at the Lord's feet listening to what he said. But Martha was distracted by all the preparations that had to be made" (Luke 10:39-40).

Mary was able to set aside her to-do list long enough to sit at Jesus' feet and focus on Him, but her manic sister Martha was too worried about table settings to be still and give Him her full attention. She was the type of chick you could count on for a casserole but wouldn't choose to hang out with at Starbucks, because you know she'd be so preoccupied scanning the room for health-code violations that she wouldn't really hear what was on your heart. Martha had the spiritual handicap of *busyness*. Mary had the God-honoring gift of *being*.

Being still and learning to focus on Jesus isn't simply a commendable feminine quality highlighted in Luke—it's a concept that's woven throughout the entirety of Scripture and is meant for all of God's children:

> *Be still, and know that I am God*; I will be exalted among the nations, I will be exalted in the earth (Psalm 46:10, emphasis added).

> The LORD your God is with you, he is mighty to save. He will take great delight in you, *he will quiet you with his love*, he will rejoice over you with singing (Zephaniah 3:17, emphasis added).

> I urge, then, first of all, that requests, prayers, intercession and thanksgiving be made for everyone—for kings and all those in authority, *that we may live peaceful and quiet lives in all godliness and holiness* (1 Timothy 2:1-2, emphasis added).

So take a deep breath, turn off your cell phone and spend some quality time with your Savior!

What's the *Story* of This Particular Book?

Paul wrote this pastoral letter to his disciple and friend Timothy as a way of passing the baton of leadership in Ephesus, a church Paul had founded. The theme of this book is "How to Run a Church 101," but it also includes affirmation regarding Timothy's character. This young man had obviously spent a great deal of time shadowing the apostle—more important, he'd spent quality time focusing on his Savior. Now Paul pronounces Tim ready to step up to the plate and succeed him!

Henrietta's Highlights on 1 Timothy

Her Synopsis

First Timothy Portrays Jesus Christ, Our Teacher

Her Suggested Bible Readings

Sunday: *Put Up a Good Fight* (1 Timothy 1)
Monday: *Pray for All Men* (1 Timothy 2)
Tuesday: *The Official Board* (1 Timothy 3)
Wednesday: *The Good Minister of Jesus Christ* (1 Timothy 4)
Thursday: *A Minister's Task* (1 Timothy 5)
Friday: *Briefing the Christian Minister* (1 Timothy 6)
Saturday: *The Whole Book* (1 Timothy 1-6)

Memorable Quotes from Dr. Mears

"Paul's charge to Timothy included more than soundness in doctrine. He wanted soundness in life."

"Godliness does not starve real living . . . Godliness is not 'goody-ness.'"

Looking for Yourself in God's Love Story

1. Read 1 Timothy 6:3-5. Some people in Paul's era—and many in ours—insist that doctrine shouldn't be an important issue for Christians—that we need to just overlook our differences and get along. What do you think?

2. Read 1 Timothy 6:6-10,17-19. Do you think these passages teach that material wealth is a "bad thing"? Why or why not? What does Paul say is more important than money?

Movie Clip Moment

When you find yourself buried by your to-do list and your heart feels like it's turned into a big ball of stress in your chest, rent *A River Runs Through It.* You don't have to really watch it, simply mute the sound and fast-forward to the fishing scenes. The stunning cinematography captures a little bit of God's beauty in creation and will help you to relax. After you exhale a few times, you might also be prompted to pray in order to express sincere gratitude for God's giving you the gift of life—that you get to wake up and muddle through one more day here on this colorful sphere we call home (at least for now)!

2 Timothy

Guarding the Good News

Several years ago at Christmastime, my friend Eva had a memorable moment with her two little girls, Abigail and Audrey. Abby, then six, was helping Eva drape garland around the piano while two-and-a-half-year-old Audrey galloped around the house playing with all the holiday decorations within her reach. Abby kept glancing toward her baby sister because Audrey had recently begun showing a keen interest in her favorite nativity set: the porcelain hand-painted one, with the "unattached" infant Messiah nestled in Mary's arms.

When Eva looked up to check on her, she noticed that Audrey looked very guilty. She was wearing a mischievous ear-to-ear grin and had her hands buried in her armpits as if she was hiding something. Then suddenly she took off running down the hall. Abby cried out, "Mama, I think she's got baby Jesus!"

Eva replied, "Well, honey, since I'm all tangled up in this garland, you're going to have to go get Him!"

Abby tore off after her sister and soon sounds like that of cats fighting were emanating from the living room. Eva got tickled listening to their scuffle and fully expected her eldest to return with a shattered ceramic Savior; but seconds later Abby came skipping merrily back down the hall and announced, "Don't worry, Mom; it's just Joseph."

Oh, if only I could be as zealous as Abby when it comes to guarding the position Immanuel should have in my heart and home!

What's the *Story* of This Particular Book?

This is the very last letter the apostle Paul wrote. He authored it while he was in a Roman prison, waiting to be executed, sometime between A.D. 64 and 68. The essence of his final message to Timothy is: *Guard the good news of the gospel of Jesus Christ!* Paul is concerned about the internal discord and external discrimination facing the New Testament Church, so he sends this literary telegram charging Timothy to protect our Messiah's message of repentance, salvation and eternal hope. He also uses this final correspondence to lovingly affirm his dear protégé.

Henrietta's Highlights on 2 Timothy

Her Synopsis

Second Timothy Portrays Jesus Christ, Our Example

Her Suggested Bible Readings

Sunday: *Stir Up Thy Gift* (2 Timothy 1:1-9)
Monday: *Hold Fast to the Truth* (2 Timothy 1:10-18)
Tuesday: *Endure Hardness as a Soldier* (2 Timothy 2:1-15)
Wednesday: *Follow Righteousness* (2 Timothy 2:16-26)
Thursday: *Know the Scriptures* (2 Timothy 3)
Friday: *Be Faithful to the End* (2 Timothy 4)
Saturday: *Receive a Crown* (1 Corinthians 9:25; 2 Timothy 4:8; James 1:12; 1 Peter 5:4; Revelation 2:10; 3:11)

Memorable Quotes from Dr. Mears

"In 2 Timothy, Paul is saying, 'Guard the testimony which is our life from God.'"

"Endure your hardships courageously and with the spirit of a hero. Don't just endure!"

Looking for Yourself in God's Love Story

Read 2 Timothy 2:1-7. Paul uses three examples—a good soldier, a good athlete and a good farmer—to illustrate intentional Christian living. Which of these three do you most identify with and why?

Movie Clip Moment

The Mission, with Jeremy Irons and Robert DeNiro, is a movie about fighting the good fight. It chronicles the battle waged by a priest (played by Jeremy Irons), his South American Indian friends and a converted former slave hunter (played intensely by Robert DeNiro) against wicked men opposed to their *mission*. This entire film will be riveting for adult viewers and includes multiple examples of guarding what is good. (There are several scenes of intense violence, so children should not be included.)

Lyrics That Lie

One of my favorite childhood memories with my sister, Theresa, centers around a silly song that included the lyrics, "Jeremiah was a bullfrog, was a good friend of mine. I never understood a single word he said, but he always had some mighty fine wine."[5]

I don't think we even understood the point of this '70s tune, but we loved the fact that the word "wine" was involved because alcohol was strictly forbidden in our house—singing it made us feel like really cool rebels! I can clearly remember the two of us sitting in Dad's truck, waiting for him to come out of a meeting, playing the bullfrog boogie over and over again on an eight-track tape one of us had gotten from somewhere. We had the windows rolled down and were belting out the lyrics as loud as we could, encouraging passersby to join in the chorus. And while we eventually got busted by Dad for "making such a racket," we were buoyed by the fact that the whole parking lot rocked with us for a few memorable minutes!

Theresa and I played that tape for months—even after it started dragging and skipping—until it eventually wore out. To this day, whenever I meet someone named Jeremiah, I usually grin and starting humming "Joy to the World" in my head. It's almost as if that song got permanently recorded in my mind! Frankly, I think we all have a mental "tape" that lyrics get imprinted on. Some of our songs are fun and harmless, like that old ode to amphibians, and some evoke warm, nostalgic memories. But some of the messages we replay do damage to our hearts.

I had lunch with a group of women recently and our conversation turned to weight. I was the only person at the table who wasn't rail-thin, and I was also the only one eating a sandwich instead of a salad *sans* dressing! Anyway, one of the petite women began to regale the rest of us with a story about how much weight she'd gained during her last pregnancy. The climax of her story was when she told us how much she weighed right before she had the baby. When she mouthed the amount, the other girls gasped in disbelief.

However, I almost choked on my sandwich: Her tipping-the-scales-before-baby weight was the exact number I'd just given the counselor at Jenny Craig as my dieting goal!

My darling lunch pals have choruses playing in their heads that tell them they're more lovable if they're lean. Their self-worth isn't securely grounded in God's love—it's partly dependent on their dress size. And most of us aren't that different. While it's our deepest desire to be accepted by our heavenly Father, we typically hear the message of His affection on tapes that skip and drag. By the time His music reaches our soul, the promises of restoration and relationship have become distorted by the lyrical lies we've chosen to believe instead.

We are so often spiritually tone-deaf.

What's the *Story* of This Particular Book?

The citizens of Crete—where one of Paul's converts, named Titus, was pastoring a church—definitely had their iPods programmed with the wrong spiritual tunes. They were tapping their toes to the heresy hummed by bad teachers, most of whom thought the gospel of grace needed an accompanying track of legalism. When Paul finds out about the discordant doctrines they are listening to, he writes this letter to emphasize God's mercy, to establish healthy parameters for church leadership and to encourage the Cretan Christians in their walk of faith.

Henrietta's Highlights on Titus

Her Synopsis
Titus Portrays Jesus Christ, Our Pattern

Her Suggested Bible Readings

Day One: *Church Officers* (Titus 1:1-9)
Day Two: *Church Enemies* (Titus 1:10-16)
Day Three: *Church Influence* (Titus 2:1-8)
Day Four: *Church Rule* (Titus 2:9-15)
Day Five: *Church Works* (Titus 3)

Memorable Quotes from Dr. Mears

"The importance of good works is stressed in this Epistle. Not that we are saved by good works, but we are saved unto good works."

"The Christian household is the main evangelizing agency everywhere."

"Be so faithful in your attitudes and obligations of life that critics of your religion will be silenced (Titus 2:8)."

Looking for Yourself in God's Love Story

1. Paul makes it clear in this letter that church leaders must first be good husbands and fathers (see Titus 1:6). How do you think someone's home life can be an accurate gauge of his or her spiritual maturity?

2. Would your family and/or friends say you act differently at church from the way you do at home? If so, how would they contrast your "Sunday self" with the real you?

3. This book gives very specific instructions to the "senior saints" of the first-century church (see Titus 2:2-5). Have you acquired more responsibility at church as you've grown in your faith? If not, can you think of a reason why? Do younger women approach you for advice that's based on biblical principles? Has anyone asked you to be his or her mentor?

Movie Clip Moment

I'm partial to movies that are based on true stories, and Disney's *Glory Road* (2006) is no exception! It's about a basketball coach named Don Haskins, who became the coach of the Texas Western Miners in 1966, his first collegiate coaching position. Young Coach Haskins was determined to mold his players into disciplined, respectable young men and hoped to win a few ball games as well. His innovative coaching philosophy ended up breaking down decades-long racial barriers in the state of Texas and affecting the national consciousness when his team made it all the way to the NCAA championship game. The way this real-life mentor taught his athletes to be honorable—regardless of the bad behavior of others—reminds me of Paul's admonition to church officers in Crete.

Winsome Friends and Influential People

For a very brief period of time, I dated a professional football player. Well, "dating" is actually a bit of a stretch—it was more like dancing at the edge of dating!

But anyway, that tiny chapter in my turbulent romantic history taught me several things. The first is that standing next to a giant guy is good for a big girl's ego. I've never felt so petite in my whole life! The second is to be careful to keep your elbows off the table when sitting next to an NFL lineman at an all-you-can-eat buffet—not so much for etiquette's sake, but to keep your body parts from being gobbled. And third, I learned what it feels like to be given special treatment purely because of someone else's position.

I'll never forget what happened one Sunday afternoon after my beau's team had just beaten the Atlanta Falcons. I was supposed to meet him outside a "private" entrance to the stadium, but I ended up being swept up with throngs of fans who'd wedged behind a barricade beside the team bus. Lots of them were holding footballs or posters for their gridiron heroes to sign—and when the players finally came striding out to board the team bus, the crowd went wild.

Suddenly my almost-boyfriend spotted me and grinned. Then he walked right over to where I was standing, lifted me up over the barrier and said, "She's with me," to the stunned security guard.

What's the *Story* of This Particular Book?

Philemon is a "He's with me" kind of book. As an old, impassioned preacher, Paul is in the position to request mercy for Onesimus, a young, runaway slave with sticky fingers. Paul is able to say, "He's with me," because he and impetuous Onesimus had become buddies in prison. And he's able to pen this letter suggesting grace for the young man when he gets out of jail because Paul knows Philemon—

the master Onesimus stole from and then deserted—from his church-planting season in Colosse. Obviously this divinely ordained friendship with an influential apostle made Onesimus a very fortunate fugitive!

Henrietta's Highlights on Philemon

Her Synopsis
Philemon Portrays Jesus Christ, Our Lord and Master

Her Suggested Bible Readings
Day One: *A Christian Gentleman* (Philemon, verses 1-7)
Day Two: *A Prisoner's Plea* (Philemon, verses 8-25)

Memorable Quotes from Dr. Mears
"Christian love and forgiveness are given prominence in this book. It shows the power of the gospel in winning a runaway thief and slave, and in changing a master's mind."

"If Paul had made slavery an issue, he would have torn society to shreds. Instead he presents principles that would surely undermine slavery and in time actually did so. Brotherhood in Christ is more than emancipation. Christianity does not merely free the slaves, but teaches them that they and their masters are one in Christ."

Looking for Yourself in God's Love Story

1. Paul pleads for Philemon to forgive Onesimus—not because he *deserves* restoration but because of Philemon's *gracious Christian character*. In other words, forgiveness was Philemon's choice. Share a recent time when you chose to forgive someone who'd wounded you.

2. Paul not only puts his reputation on the line for a former bad boy, but he also incurs Onesimus's debt when he says, "Charge it to me" (see Philemon, verse 18).

Apart from Jesus, has anyone ever paid a significant debt on your behalf? If so, how did you respond to your benefactor? Have you expressed your gratitude again recently?

Movie Clip Moment

Schindler's List (1993) is an Academy Award, Golden Globe and Grammy winning movie based on the book *Schindler's Ark* by Thomas Keneally. Steven Spielberg directed this gripping true story about a successful businessman named Oskar Schindler, who—compelled by compassion—used his influence to shelter people in need, much like Paul gave shelter to Onesimus. Schindler saved the lives of over 1,000 Jewish people during the Holocaust. If you haven't already watched this film, prepare to be disturbed by scenes of unspeakable cruelty. But also look forward to being deeply moved by scenes of true kindness. I think it's a great movie for families with older kids to view and then process questions about how we as Christians should respond in situations in which people are being mistreated, abused or even murdered.

Adversity Makes the Heart Grow Fonder

I read a story recently about a little-known hero of the faith named Thomas Chalmers. He was born in 1780, in the small fishing community of Anstruther, Scotland. He grew up in a poor family—one in which he was likely served fish sticks too often for supper—but one in which knowledge was highly valued. And before most children had mastered potty training, wee Master Chalmers's brilliance had bobbed to the surface. By the age of 3, he could read both Greek and Hebrew. By the age of 10, he'd read every single book in the village where he lived with his mother, father and 13 brothers and sisters.

Long before he started shaving, Thomas Chalmers was packed off to St. Andrews University. He finished his studies—getting advanced degrees in mathematics and theology—by the age of 19. And by the time he was 20, he was hired to be both a math professor at St. Andrews and the pastor of a small rural parish.

Some would argue that the mental aptitude of a man like Chalmers is as rare as a happy skinny woman. (I think grouchiness can often be linked to a lack of carbohydrates.) However, the enormity of his cognitive awareness stood in stark contrast to his heart awareness. In spite of his intellect, he didn't "get" grace. He acted more like a jerk than like Jesus. He came across as arrogant and condescending and much more interested in *ideas* than *individuals*. One biographer says of Chalmers at this stage in his life that he was "widely admired, but universally disliked!"

Thus, God gave young Tom a providential time-out. After witnessing the premature deaths of two siblings from tuberculosis, Tom himself got very sick as well. He was bedridden for months and came close to kicking the proverbial bucket. It was in that weak posture that this gifted young man finally fell in love with His Savior. He realized that in his obsessive quest for knowledge *about* God and His creation, he'd forfeited an intimate relationship with the Lover of his soul. Once he turned his attention to the heavenly Father's unmerited kindness, he became a totally different man.

When he finally recovered his physical health, Chalmers gave up his distinguished university position so as to pour himself into his county parish. He spent three days every week walking the countryside to visit people—whether they attended his church or not! His life became characterized by the language of love. By the time of his death in 1847, Thomas Chalmers had pioneered an enormous and effective outreach to the poor and underprivileged. He had also helped build and pay for at least 500 new churches, initiated the construction and funding of more than 400 new schools, and had trained and deployed over 800 missionaries to foreign lands.

He explained his transformation from supercilious professor to compassionate pastor as *the expulsive power of the new affection.* Chalmers insisted that when we recognize the enormity of the gospel and really connect with Christ, that new love will "crowd out" lesser affections. When we begin to understand how amazing God's grace is, our response to His love will expel the illegitimate squatters in our soul. Real relationship with Jesus *will* change us from the inside out.

What's the *Story* of This Particular Book?

Much like He did in Dr. Chalmers's life, God used *suffering* to shape the first-century Jewish believers in Jesus (hence, the name of the book: *Hebrews*!). They had been struggling with severe political and social persecution because of their faith and were thus being tempted to revert back to Judaism-without-Jesus. So God speaks through their pastor, to remind them of the supremacy of the Messiah: how Jesus is *better* than the Law, the Prophets, angels, Moses and the Jewish priesthood. He tells them that Jesus is the only "hero" with shoulders broad enough to carry their burdens; how Jesus is also an empathetic hero, one who has experienced every hardship they could ever face. And in light of these truths, the writer of Hebrews encourages these weary believers to keep on keeping on!

Henrietta's Highlights on Hebrews

Her Synopsis
Hebrews Portrays Jesus Christ, Our Intercessor at the Throne

Her Suggested Bible Readings

Sunday: *Christ, Superior to Prophets and Angels* (Hebrews 1)
Monday: *Christ, Superior to Moses* (Hebrews 3)
Tuesday: *Christ, Superior to Aaron* (Hebrews 5)
Wednesday: *Christ's Superior Covenants* (Hebrews 8)
Thursday: *Christ's Superior Atonement* (Hebrews 10:1-25)
Friday: *Christ's Superior Faith Life* (Hebrews 11)
Saturday: *Christ's Superior Privileges* (Hebrews 12–13)

Memorable Quotes from Dr. Mears

"We as Christians have that which is better—better in every way. The key word to the book of Hebrews is 'better.'"

"This book has been called the fifth Gospel. The four describe Christ's ministry on earth; this one describes His ministry in heaven at God's right hand."

"When God wanted to save us from our sin, He did not send an angel, but His Son. God came not in the form of an angel, but in the form of a man. He became Man to redeem man."

Looking for Yourself in God's Love Story

1. Christians in the first century were considered a small, minority sect within Judaism, until a large (and vocal) number of Jews let it be known that they didn't want to be associated with those "weirdos who believe that Jesus Christ is the Messiah!" Has anyone ever assumed you believed something you don't or lumped you in with a group of Christians that you disagree with? If so, how did you respond?

2. Read Hebrews 2:1-4. Spiritual "drifting" refers to behavior that's not overtly corrupt yet still diverts our attention from God. What are the biggest distractions in your life right now?

3. Read Hebrews 4:1-11. Have you done something recently you knew displeased God, and then have you tossed and turned at night as a result? How would you describe the relationship between *rebellion* and *rest*?

4. Read Hebrews 13:1-3, John 13:34-35 and 3 John 1:5-8. Why do you think a commitment to hospitality was a *necessity* for Early Christian missionaries? Do you think hospitality is as important in modern-day evangelistic efforts? Why or why not?

Movie Clip Moment

The first time I watched *Remember the Titans*, I couldn't help but think of Hebrews! Both "teams" endured hardship and grew much stronger and much more cohesive as a result. Plus, the coaches of both teams were fantastic motivators, encouraging their charges to press on, persevere and keep their eyes on the prize. This is one of the few recent films wholesome enough for the whole family—and one that naturally leads to a pertinent Bible lesson when the popcorn's gone!

A Divine Appointment in a Dodge Van

I had a heartwarming experience in America's heartland recently. Several friends and I had the privilege of sharing at a large Christian women's conference, and when the program ended, we decided to go to dinner together to essentially exhale and celebrate. Someone told us there was a great Mexican restaurant in town, so we asked the hotel bellman to call a big cab because there were seven of us and not one rental car. Of course, we didn't know the restaurant was *way* across town and the taxi fare would be larger than our dinner tab!

However, no one complained because we were just happy to be sitting down and delighted with how the day had gone. We laughed and talked through lots of chips and salsa and generous south-of-the-border portions until our stomachs were stretched and our eyelids were heavy. We groaned away from the table and wearily trudged outside, ready to get back to the hotel and get some sleep before having to get up early to catch our return flights.

Unfortunately, the cab company wasn't what you'd call accommodating. Or prompt. We waited and waited and then waited some more. After several pleading phone calls, a dilapidated van finally pulled to the curb in front of the restaurant, driven by a rather large, very intimidating-looking woman. It was also immediately obvious that her rattletrap only had room for five people—not seven like the grouchy dispatcher said!

But desperate people do desperate things, and our driver didn't look like the type to tangle with, so we somehow wedged ourselves in. We rolled along in claustrophobic silence for a few minutes and then—as if we suddenly remembered we were Christians—someone asked the driver what her name was—which led to questions about her life. Pretty soon Christina's story came tumbling out. She had two kids, a boy and a girl. Both had been murdered in the past few years in gang-related incidents. Her daughter had been 20 when she died and her son had been 24.

Christina told us that she now took care of her two grandchildren and how she hoped to make a better life for them. When we asked what kept her going through such a difficult season, she said in a tired voice, "I just try to keep my eyes on the Lord and trust Him to take care of us." Well, that triggered a chorus of agreement from us, and after several stories about God's faithfulness, we started praying out loud for her. And that group prayer turned into a mini-revival. By the time we pulled up to the hotel we were all in tears, awestruck by God's presence among us. Then we shared a very emotional goodbye in front of a wide-eyed hotel lobby audience. I guess seeing a group of lily-white people hugging and kissing one big, tattooed African American woman is a bit unusual!

However strange it might have seemed, we knew that our meeting was as providential as it was precious. We're absolutely convinced that God orchestrated our paths to cross Christina's on that incredible Kansas night.

> Therefore confess your sins to each other and pray for each other so that you may be healed. The prayer of a righteous man [or woman] is powerful and effective (James 5:16).

What's the *Story* of This Particular Book?

James has been subtitled "the Proverbs of the New Testament" because of its practical, application-oriented style. The letter was most likely written by Jesus' brother, James, who didn't profess faith in Jesus' deity until after His death on the cross. Thus, there's a certain sobriety to James's narrative. He emphasizes the fact that there will be suffering and difficulty in this life. And James certainly faced hardship—he was ultimately hurled to his death because he wouldn't renounce his faith in Jesus as the Messiah. James also accentuates the importance of "walking your talk"—of how faith must be accompanied by deeds. In other words, if you're a Christian, your life will prove it.

Henrietta's Highlights on James

Her Synopsis
James Portrays Jesus Christ, Our Pattern

Her Suggested Bible Readings

Sunday: *Faith Tested* (James 1:1-21)
Monday: *Faith Lived Out* (James 1:22-27)
Tuesday: *Faith and Brotherhood* (James 2:1-13)
Wednesday: *Faith Dead Without Works* (James 2:14-26)
Thursday: *Faith and Tongue Control* (James 3)
Friday: *Faith Rebukes Worldliness* (James 4)
Saturday: *Faith in Prayer* (James 5)

Memorable Quotes from Dr. Mears

"Paul dwells on the source of our faith. James tells of the fruit of our faith. One lays the foundations in Christ; the other builds the superstructure. Christ is both 'author and finisher' of our faith."

"Valueless is the character that knows no testing. There is a joy of overcoming. There is no greater satisfaction than to know we have resisted temptation victoriously."

"Tradition tells us that on his death they discovered that his knees were worn hard as a camel's through his constant habit of prayer."

"Works do not save us, but they are a pretty good evidence that we are saved."

Looking for Yourself in God's Love Story

1. A friend of mine (Sheila Walsh) says, "Some of God's best gifts are wrapped in boxes that make your hands bleed when you open them"—which seems to echo James's premise about suffering. What's the most wonderful yet painful present God's given you recently?

2. Read James 3:1-12. In one sentence, how would you summarize this convicting "sermon"?

3. It's been said that the basic theology for believers is found in James 5:13. Do you agree with that assessment?

Movie Clip Moment

In the film *Liar, Liar,* rubber-faced attorney Jim Carrey epitomizes a life lived *saying* one thing but *doing* something different altogether. And while it's billed as a comedy, there's a very serious message in this movie about the importance of having a walk that matches your talk. People can promise all kinds of things, but unless their motives correspond with their monologue, it's pretty much just hot air!

Lions, Tigers and Lincolns, Oh My!

I went through a "mini" midlife crisis last year and became the proud owner of a black motorcycle. My insurance premiums shot up, along with a lot of church eyebrows. However, I like the fact that riding a motorcycle is not a stereotypical hobby for most Southern female Bible teachers. I've got just enough "rebel" in me to want to buck convention and bend the rules a bit! Plus, I'm learning some great life lessons.

For instance, when I'm riding my motorcycle, I notice little things that I never noticed in a car. Little things like: gravel in the road, oil spots, dogs with bad attitudes, and blue-haired ladies in big American cars. Daydreaming isn't a good idea when you're next to a retiree who's piloting a Mercury Grand Marquis. I always smile at big-car drivers, give them the right-of-way and watch them like a hawk, because you never know when one of them is going to accidentally squash you like a bug!

A few weeks ago, I had a close call. An AARP airhead didn't stop at a red light and zoomed right in front of me in her land-yacht. Thankfully I was paying attention. I stopped well in front of the path of destruction and thanked God for allowing me to see her coming. That near-miss reminded me once again of how very important it is to watch where we're going, literally and spiritually.

Recently a friend who prays for me on a regular basis told me that she's been praying *one thing* for me over and over again. I asked her what she'd been so compelled to pray for—secretly hoping she was putting all that energy into my "future husband" or a "future major weight loss"—but then she told me she's been praying for me to *be alert*. I have to admit, I was a little disappointed. Being alert has never been a great aspiration for me.

But as the months have passed, I've become so grateful for her request on my behalf. I've been really busy this past season—bombarded is more accurate—and have felt myself being too distracted to pay close attention to my surroundings.

It's surprising how quickly sin slides into a preoccupied life. I've justified watching movies that normally would make me blush, I've let my mouth run ahead of my wisdom, and I've spent far too little time alone with the Lover of my soul. I've become woefully "alert deficient." Alertness is an asset we should all pray for . . . because distraction can lead to being devoured! "Be self-controlled and alert. Your enemy the devil prowls around like a roaring lion looking for someone to devour" (1 Peter 5:8).

What's the *Story* of This Particular Book?

Peter—the disciple most likely to put his foot in his mouth when he was younger—penned this letter to the first-century Christian community. To say they had a few difficulties is a fantastic understatement: They were scattered across Europe, persecuted by just about everybody and were plagued with infighting. Peter's message is partly encouraging—he basically tells them that their struggles will work like a spiritual immunization shot, galvanizing them against the full sickness of sin and temptation. His message is also a warning—Peter sounds the trumpet for New Testament believers to be on the lookout for Satan, our greatest enemy, who is always lurking in the darkness ready to pounce on the preoccupied.

Henrietta's Highlights on 1 Peter

Her Synopsis

First Peter Portrays Jesus Christ, Precious Cornerstone of Our Faith

Her Suggested Bible Readings

Sunday: *Precious Faith* (1 Peter 1:1-12)
Monday: *Precious Blood* (1 Peter 1:13-25)
Tuesday: *Precious Cornerstone* (1 Peter 2:1-10)
Wednesday: *Precious Savior* (1 Peter 2:11-25)
Thursday: *Precious Is a Meek and Quiet Spirit* (1 Peter 3)
Friday: *Precious Suffering of Christ* (1 Peter 4)
Saturday: *Precious Crowns* (1 Peter 5)

Memorable Quotes from Dr. Mears

"In the Gospels we see Peter, the impulsive, restless soul, sometimes fearless but again a coward, even going as far as to deny his Lord with a curse! In his own Epistles we see him patient, restful, and loving, and having a courage purified and strengthened by the indwelling Spirit. This is a wonderful illustration of the transforming work of God in a human life."

"A greenhouse religion is of very little value to others. It is good for us to be compelled to justify our faith before our fellow humans."

"The Christian life is like a jungle battle. Peter tells us who our enemy is. He is the devil. His work is opposed to all that is good in this world. He is pictured as a roaring lion, seeking his prey . . . he is watching for the vulnerable spot, for the unguarded door to our hearts."

Looking for Yourself in God's Love Story

1. Dr. Mears encourages us to read 1 Peter in one sitting and highlight every mention of the words "joy," "grace," "glory" and "suffering." After completing this exercise, how would you describe the relationship among those words?

2. In this book, Peter gives a basic behavioral guide—*control your tongue, do good, don't fight* and *pursue peace*—for believers to follow when they find themselves in trouble. What terms would you use to describe Peter's behavior when he found himself "in trouble" in the Garden of Gethsemane and in the hours leading up to the crucifixion? What one adjective would you use to describe the difference between Peter the young disciple and Peter the mature believer?

3. In light of Peter's transformation, what terms would you use to describe how you have changed, from the time you first trusted in Jesus as your Savior to the woman you are today?

4. Besides "roaring lion," what other biblical images best describe Satan's poisonous personality and murderous intent? What are some practical ways we can be on guard?

Movie Clip Moment

The Ghost and the Darkness (1996) is based on a true story about two man-eating, rogue lions that terrorized an African village in the late 1800s. The cinematography is incredible and the musical score is suspenseful (not unlike that other scary animal movie, *Jaws*), but what makes this film especially spooky is knowing that the drama depicted on celluloid actually took place. More than 100 people really were killed by these two lions, whom natives began calling The Ghost and The Darkness. Watching this movie will give you a healthy respect for wild lions; more important, it will give you an unforgettable—and biblical—image of what the devil is like. While you're cowering on the couch watching it, think about ways in which the villagers could have guarded themselves more effectively, and imagine what the spiritual parallels to those "lion safeguards" would be.

2 PETER

Beware, These Guppies Bite

Several years ago I went on a 10-day "adventure" vacation to Belize, Central America, with my friend Julie. Both of us had dreamed of visiting the tropical paradise of Belize for years, and we couldn't wait to go diving in a place called Shark and Ray Alley. "But no worries"—I explained to my worried mother on the phone—the sharks in Shark and Ray Alley are nurse sharks, which aren't typically dangerous. They have small mouths and their bite radius isn't big enough to sever an adult human appendage. And of course, leaving Belize in one piece was high on our vacation wish list!

Soon after our arrival, we found a local diving guide (whose name was prominently tattooed across his generous tummy) to take us out to swim with the sharks. He flashed us a gold-toothed grin and promised us an afternoon to remember. However, on the way to the dive site, "Goldie" warned us not to get our fingers near the sharks' mouths because they can't distinguish human hands from the squid they're fed. He emphasized this warning by gesturing toward his shy son's hands, which were missing a few fingers. Julie and I gave each other worried glances, wondering if we'd bitten off more than we could chew (no pun intended)!

But as soon as the boat idled up to our destination, my apprehension was replaced by amazement. Right in front of us was a surreal scene of shark fins slicing through water dotted with neon snorkels. I quickly flopped backward out of the boat, with an underwater camera in my hand and my heart in my throat. The moment my mask cleared, I saw sharks gliding past me in every direction. I was so dazed by the sight I forgot to breathe for a minute or so. I did remember to keep my hands balled into fists, though, because I'd suddenly grown very fond of my fingers!

In much the same way, as Christians, we have to beware of the man-eaters lurking in our neighborhoods: the superficial girls who distract us with gossip in small group, the slick televangelist who promises our dreams will come true if we'll just write him a big check, the "Bible teacher" who passionately emphasizes her prejudice over God's Word. *Anyone* who hawks religion instead of a relationship with Jesus will take a bite out of our souls if we don't stay alert.

We need to really listen to what persuasive preachers are promoting to make sure it matches up with what the gospel teaches. We need to take a careful look before we leap into unfamiliar spiritual waters.

What's the *Story* of This Particular Book?

Dear old Pete wrote this pastoral letter to warn naïve young Christians about the religious sharks prowling up and down the pews. In the second half of the first century, there were lots of false prophets preying on immature believers. This spiritual shepherd uses loving language to encourage his flock, calling them "brothers [and sisters]" and "dear friends" (2 Peter 1:10; 3:14), but he sure doesn't mince words when he describes those who've turned their back on the truth, calling them "dogs" and "pigs" (2 Peter 2:22)! And though he's languishing in a hellish Roman prison while writing this note, he still enthuses about heaven–it's as if the promise of his eternal home is what's keeping him going.

Henrietta's Highlights on 2 Peter

Her Synopsis

Second Peter Portrays Jesus Christ, Our Strength

Her Suggested Bible Readings

Sunday: *Christian Virtues* (2 Peter 1:1-14)
Monday: *Christ's Word Exalted* (2 Peter 1:15-21)
Tuesday: *Christless Teachers* (2 Peter 2:1-14)
Wednesday: *Christ Against the Backslider* (2 Peter 2:15-22)
Thursday: *Christ's Coming Scoffed* (2 Peter 3:1-9)
Friday: *Christ's Coming Assured* (2 Peter 3:10-18)
Saturday: *Christ Our Hope* (2 Peter 1–3)

Memorable Quotes from Dr. Mears

"Shallow knowledge makes superficial Christians."

"Peter, like Paul, warns Christians from standing still. Don't remain babes in Christ, tripping over every teaching, but grow strong."

"God can only do one thing with these kinds of teachers, and that is to destroy them. 'Light that is trifled with becomes lightning.'"

"What lives we ought to live while we wait for His coming!"

Looking for Yourself in God's Love Story

1. Read 2 Peter 1:3-9. In what specific ways have you grown in your relationship with Jesus over the past year? What do you think the people closest to you would say is the biggest spiritual change they've seen in you?
2. Read 2 Peter 2:1-3,12-14,18-19. In light of this passage, what adjectives would you use to describe a false prophet?
3. Read 2 Peter 3:1-13 and Matthew 25:1-13. What's the common theme of these passages? On a barely related note, what's the most unattractive bridesmaid dress you've ever had to wear?

Movie Clip Moment

Deep Blue Sea is a silly but suspenseful B-grade movie about really big, really scary, really angry sharks. This film has way too many expletives in the dialogue, so I don't recommend a full viewing (though there is a token Christian character–played convincingly by rapper L. L. Cool J–who actually has a good personality and isn't a mean-spirited, judgmental idiot!). If you use your mute button and fast forward to the "chase" scenes, you can find some very effective illustrations of predatory prophets. And since you aren't going to watch the whole thing, I'll tell you that the Christian guy outsmarts the mean fish and makes it out alive!

There's a Whole Lotta Lovin' Goin' On!

One of my favorite women in the world is my best friend's mom, Michele Hill. She lives in Memphis, Tennessee, and takes "Southern hospitality" to a whole new level. Michele runs her home kind of like a "humane society" for people—she adopts "strays" of all kinds! She helps them get settled, introduces them to a Bible study and surrounds them with love and support. But, of course, unlike the real Humane Society, she doesn't euthanize her guests when they stay too long!

Kim says her mom and dad (who has since passed away) took in brokenhearted boarders for as long as she can remember. She said it wasn't at all unusual for her to come home from school and find that someone had moved into her room for a week or two (or three or four). And while she didn't always appreciate getting the boot from her own bedroom, she admired her parents' compassionate generosity, especially when she got older.

After college, Kim moved to Nashville to pursue a career in music, and she soon met a young guy named José. He was a relatively new Christian, earnestly trying to honor God, but struggling with many issues from his past. After hearing his story, Kim immediately thought her parents could help, so she called her mom and explained the situation. Michele listened intently as Kim poured out José's saga and then responded, "Of course, he can stay here, Kim! Tell him to head to Memphis and I'll start getting a room ready."

Several hours later there was a knock at the door of the Hill house and Michele opened it to find a young, clean-cut Hispanic man standing there. She quickly leaned forward and hugged him, saying, "We're so glad you're finally here! Please come in—our home is your home!" But he just stood there rigidly. Michele thought, *Poor little guy. He doesn't even know how to respond to kindness.*

So she leaned forward a second time and hugged him even harder, repeating her greeting. But he remained unresponsive and seemed very wary.

As she was releasing him from the second squeeze, Michele looked down and noticed a silver, metal canister by his side. Then over his shoulder, she noticed a white truck with a familiar logo in the driveway. It was only then that Kim's mom finally realized she was embracing the pest-control guy! He wasn't José—he was the terrified Terminex man!

Even when she grabs the wrong guy, Michele's motive is a good one. The *open arms* approach is her way of living out the gospel, because she's convinced that part of our responsibility as believers is to reach out to those around us who are in need. Which brings to mind a convicting question posed in the book of 1 John: "If anyone has material possessions and sees his brother in need but has no pity on him, how can the love of God be in him?" (3:17).

Now I'm not suggesting that we all run out and passionately squeeze the pest-control men in our lives, but I do think this world would be a much better place if we hugged more and hoarded less, if those of us who claim the name of Christ would be committed to sharing our stuff—especially with those in need.

What's the *Story* of This Particular Book?

The main purpose of this short and sensitive letter is to encourage Christians in their relationship with Jesus and to assure them of the eternal life they'll certainly share with their Savior. John's (who's probably almost 90 years old when he writes this) compassion for doubting believers is evident in his choice of words—but he's also quite dogmatic about the need for believers to "flesh out" their faith. He holds up three key indicators that prove whether someone has truly put his or her trust in Christ: a *moral* factor (see 1 John 2:3-6), a *relational* factor (see 1 John 4:7-8) and a *doctrinal* factor (see 1 John 1:5–2:6; 4:1-4; 5:5). He essentially explains that *if* God lives in your heart, He'll stick out and others will notice!

Henrietta's Highlights on 1 John

Her Synopsis
First John Portrays Jesus Christ, Our Life

Her Suggested Bible Readings
Day One: *Walking in Fellowship* (1 John 1:1–2:14)
Day Two: *Walking as Children of God* (1 John 2:15–3)
Day Three: *Walking in Love* (1 John 4)
Day Four: *Walking in Knowledge* (1 John 5)

Memorable Quotes from Dr. Mears
"He wrote his Epistle that those who believe in Christ might KNOW that they have eternal life (1 John 5:13)."

"John says we not only must believe like Christians, but we also must act like Christians."

"We can have confidence when we know Christ. John uses the word 'know' more than forty times in his Epistles. Trust Christianity is more than a creed—it is something that can be known and felt."

Looking for Yourself in God's Love Story

1. Read through 1 John in one sitting. In one sentence, how would you summarize John's main theme?

2. Underline the word "know" every time it appears in 1 John. Which of the "knows" most resonates with you? Which of the "knows" would you like to be more confident in?

3. First John 1:8-9 proclaims the tender promise of God's *absolute* forgiveness. What past sin do you have the most difficult time believing that God has really forgiven you for? Write out verse 9 on a note card, personalize it (i.e.,

replace the word "sin" with the specific action you have the hardest time receiving God's forgiveness for), and place it someplace where you'll see it often—like your car visor or bedside table.

4. Do you have a "Michele" in your life—someone who, for the sake of Christ, gives often and freely to those in need? Think about inviting him or her out for coffee (or simply write a note) so as to affirm that person's generous spirit toward others.

Movie Clip Moment

I rarely recommend movies that I haven't seen, but given the fact that it's not playing in Nashville yet, I'll make an exception with *Mother Teresa*. Several respected Christian leaders and ministries have given it a "thumbs-up," plus a large portion of the proceeds from ticket sales are going to Christ-centered charities such as Samaritan's Purse, Compassion and Childcare International. Therefore, I think it's a safe bet! This movie wasn't produced by Hollywood, but by a group of Italians who hired little-known actors (with the notable exception of Olivia Hussey, who portrays Mother Teresa). From what I've heard, this film paints an exceptional portrait of compassion. It depicts how one single woman—motivated purely by love—affected the hearts and souls of so many others.

Company That Corrupts

I've always been outdoorsy and adventuresome, but I tend to bite off more than I can chew—or more than my companions can chew! Most of my friends have stories of misadventures with me: My friend Kim suffered a shoulder injury after following me off a ski jump, my friend Sarah broke her collarbone when we went mountain biking together, to name a few. But my aunt Darlene probably suffered the worst on an outing I talked her into several years ago.

She and her husband, Dale, and my much younger cousins Steven and Sarah drove across the country from Central Florida to Arizona based on my gushing description of a recent, *easy* hike I'd taken down the Havasupi Trail in the Grand Canyon. I'd enthusiastically told Darlene that the trip would be *perfect* for their family vacation. Thus, as they zoomed along the Interstate toward our rendezvous point (I was driving down from Colorado to meet them), the four of them talked excitedly about the red rock formations they'd get to climb and the iridescent waterfall they were going to splash in. But they weren't expecting the place to be so desolate. I'd forgotten to tell them that there weren't any restaurants or gas stations or bathrooms within about 50 miles of where we were starting our trek. Not even a vending machine or porta-potty. Because the route is located on a federal Indian reservation, there are no commercial entities at the trailhead, and only horses and humans are allowed to walk in and out.

Eight hours later, after trudging through what seemed to be a never-ending path of rock and sand, we reached our campsite. Sarah's feet were blistered, Darlene's shoulders were rubbed raw from the backpack straps, and the tent they'd rented and erected was tiny—much too small for their whole family. Plus, it was miserably hot—like a giant, gritty furnace. The last time I'd hiked the Canyon had been in the winter when the weather was balmy and breezy. I hadn't stopped to think how different it might be in July! I tried to enliven our sullen crew by luring them to the aforementioned waterfall. I thought a relaxing swim in the glorious blue water would cool us off and bring back the love. I didn't know the waterfall dried up and turned into a dinky, tepid trickle during the summer season.

I didn't think things could get any worse until Darlene unpacked "dinner." I'd encouraged her to bring lots of string cheese—because it's easy to pack and provides protein—along with chocolate-covered granola bars and fruit—because they'd replenish the calories we had expended. When I watched her face fall as she scooped the gooey, inedible mess out of the bottom of her backpack, I felt like a big, fat sadist. I just knew they were going to be emotionally scarred for life!

To make a very long saga shorter, I had to abandon them and hike away early the next morning because I had to go back to work. And then things spiraled from bad to terrible. Dale had a heat stroke—which a sleep-deprived and discombobulated Darlene misdiagnosed as a heart attack. In her panicky state, she flagged down a passing Havasu native on horseback and tearfully bribed him to carry eight-year-old Sarah out of the Canyon. She told me later that watching that man ride off with her youngest child was one of the most difficult things she's ever done.

When they *finally* got back to their Flagstaff hotel, sunburned and starving but otherwise physically sound, Steven accidentally turned on the heat instead of the air-conditioning. Darlene said she was so exhausted that she just laid there sweating, wondering if heat stroke was a contagious condition and pondering how in a cruel twist of fate—after miraculously making it out of the Grand Canyon alive—they were going to meet their Maker in the Marriott!

Needless to say, she adamantly refuses to go on another Grand Canyon hike with me and researches my recommendations on the Internet now before agreeing to join in my adventures. My company on that camping trip simply caused her too much agony!

What's the *Story* of This Particular Book?

Gentle John wrote this short note (2 and 3 John have the distinction of being the shortest books in the New Testament, each containing fewer than 300 Greek words) to a certain Christian woman and her family. After some opening words of appreciation, the letter contains a strong warning not to extend hospitality to false prophets or to trust their smooth talking and be duped. It's one thing to be sincere in offering welcome, but beware devious people who want nothing but to exploit Christian kindness. John advises this Christian woman that the false teachers she has received in her home are wolves in sheep's clothing, threatening to destroy the Church with their terrible theology.

Henrietta's Highlights on 2 John

Her Synopsis
Second John Portrays Jesus Christ, the Truth

Her Suggested Bible Readings
Day One: *Walking in Truth* (2 John, verses 1-13)

Memorable Quotes from Dr. Mears
"This is the only book in the Bible addressed to a woman."

"We must test all the teachings in the world by the Scriptures 'for the truth's sake' (2 John 2). This is the final test. Test your experience by the Word of God, but never test the Word of God by your experience!"

Looking for Yourself in God's Love Story

1. Read 2 John, verse 12. Contrast John's temperament here with that which is suggested by the nickname given to him and his brother James (see Mark 3:17).

2. Read 2 John, verses 9-10. Why do you think it's so important not to bring false prophets *into your home*? Do you think it's okay to relate to false prophets *outside* your home, say in the workplace?

3. Do you think there should be a difference between how we connect with non-Christians and how we connect with non-Christian *leaders*? Why or why not?

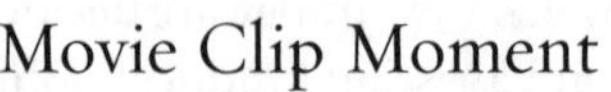

Movie Clip Moment

The humorous and nostalgic movie *A Christmas Story* chronicles the story of a little boy named Ralphie who desperately wants a B.B. gun for Christmas. The narration is often over-the-top—but very funny. And one of the most memorable scenes takes place when one little boy listens to another and ends up with his tongue stuck to a frozen flagpole! This film clip provides a light-hearted look at why we shouldn't trust *everything* people tell us!

The Subversive Power of Subtle Sin

My dogs—darling Jack Russell terriers named Harley and Dottie—love to give me presents. I can always tell when they've procured something by the way they prance around, wagging their tails, literally leading me to their offering. Sometimes they've caught a bird that flew too close to the ground. Once they managed to capture a field mouse and hold him hostage until I got home to admire their "present." But their usual gift is a dead mole that they've tenaciously pursued by digging holes all over the yard!

While I don't normally encourage my pets' homicidal tendencies, I must admit that I don't lose any sleep over their war on moles, because I can't stand the near-sighted little varmints! They tunnel their way through my flowerbeds, gorge themselves on my perennial bulbs, wreak havoc on my rare hostas and leave unsightly ridges in their wake. Thus, when I see one of those furry scoundrels curled up in a death pose, all I can think is, *Good riddance!*

I think secret sin is much like one of those sightless pests. You might not notice it at first, because rebellion can burrow under the surface of a friendship or a family or a community of believers for a season, but eventually the damage caused by hidden disobedience will show up. Hearts will be crushed and trust will be compromised. Therefore, honesty is *always* the best policy. Habits that flourish in the dark will die when we pull them into the light.

The next time you feel sin tunneling in your soul or see its telltale scars in the garden of someone you love, pursue it with compassionate candor and tenacious prayer!

What's the *Story* of This Particular Book?

The original addressee of John's third epistle was a gentleman named Gaius, a supporter of itinerant New Testament missionaries. While praising Gaius's character, John also warns about the insubordinate behavior of another guy named Diotrephes (see 3 John, verses 9-10). He was a real stinker who was tunneling through the Church, creating division, spreading lies and causing nothing but trouble.

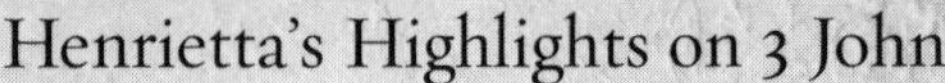

Henrietta's Highlights on 3 John

Her Synopsis
Jesus Christ, the Way

Her Suggested Bible Reading
Day One: *Walking in the Way* (3 John, verses 1-14)

Memorable Quotes from Dr. Mears
"Gaius was noted for his loving hospitality. John urges him to continue entertaining the traveling preachers in spite of bitter opposition of an autocratic and blustering church official named Diotrephes."

"You can be either a Gaius, helping in the kingdom, or a Diotrephes, hindering the cause."

Looking for Yourself in God's Love Story

1. Do you think *going* on mission trips is more important than playing a part in *sending* others?

2. Who is the most hospitable Christian you know? Do you think other people would characterize you as hospitable? Why or why not?

Movie Clip Moment

An amazing film, *Walk the Line* tells the true story of the "Man in Black" (Johnny Cash). It's one of my favorite flicks—very redemptive and inspirational. The main themes of this movie are Johnny's enduring relationship with June Carter Cash and his dramatic journey into and out of drug addiction. But there's also a priceless, humorous scene in which his soon-to-be in-laws (June's mom and dad) work together to run off a destructive, drug-dealing "mole."

Missing the Messiah

Nashville is commonly referred to as Music City, and I can vouch for the fact that this hilly Southern hamlet is full of musicians. You can't throw a rock without hitting someone trying to make it in the recording industry! It seems like most of the waiters and waitresses around here are hopeful vocalists, guitarists or songwriters, simply waiting to be discovered.

In our church alone, we've got scores of professional musicians. Some are quite famous, and some are quietly hoping that someone besides their mama will buy their CD. One of my favorites among the vocational artists is a man named Charlie Peacock.

Charlie's pretty well known in music circles. He's recorded something like 15 personal projects and has produced multiple others, including Switchfoot, Audio Adrenaline, Al Green and CeCe Winans to name a few. He's also won just about every award imaginable and was named by Billboard's *Encyclopedia of Record Producers* as one of the 500 most important record producers in music history.[6] He's also written several books about art, authenticity, worship and God. Suffice it to say, Charlie's a pretty big deal.

But he's also disarmingly humble. I get to take seminary classes with Charlie and his wife, Andi, and you'd never know he was a celebrated musician, given his unassuming behavior. So it was delightful to watch a woman in our class approach him yesterday morning after seeing him perform at a church concert the night before. She walked up to him—kind of wide-eyed—and explained that she didn't even know he could sing or play the piano until watching him "do his thing" on stage. She paused for just a moment and then blurted out enthusiastically, "I didn't know you were *you*!"

You know the same thing could be said for the way most of the world has viewed Jesus throughout history: Most people don't recognize that He is . . . well, who He is. Jesus—Joseph's son-turned-traveling-evangelist—was actually *Immanuel*, God with us. Most people miss the Messiah. Most people glance right past the Lamb of God, failing to see that He is the only One capable of loving them perfectly, that He is the One their hearts are so hungry for.

What's the *Story* of This Particular Book?

Most of the people living in the second half of the first century didn't realize that Jesus was the Messiah. It certainly didn't help that Roman authorities ridiculed Christianity and that heretics from within the Church were distracting believers from seeing who He really was. Jesus' half-brother Jude pens this letter, charging believers to really recognize their Redeemer and live in light of that vision. When you consider that Jude came to faith in Christ only after His death and resurrection—Jude *lived* with Jesus and still didn't realize He was Immanuel—it makes sense that he would be so passionate about helping others comprehend Jesus' deity.

Henrietta's Highlights on Jude

Her Synopsis
Jesus Christ, Our Keeper

Her Suggested Bible Reading
Day One: *Walking Without Falling* (Jude, verses 1-25)

Memorable Quote from Dr. Mears
"Second Peter and Jude are very similar in thought and language. Both men were dealing with the dangers confronting the doctrines of the Church."

Looking for Yourself in God's Love Story

Read Jude's doxology (see verses 24-25). How has God kept *you* from falling recently?

Movie Clip Moment

The Notebook is a tearjerker of a love story (based on Nicholas Sparks's best-selling novel and starring James Garner, Gena Rowlands, Ryan Gosling, Rachel McAdams and Joan Allen) that shifts back and forth from the past to the present. Near the end of the movie there's a poignant scene between the elderly lovebirds Noah and Allie (played by James and Gena) in which she doesn't recognize who he really is. This clip is a powerful illustration of how we sometimes completely miss a person's significance in our life.

Wide-Eyed Wonder

Recently I sat near a little boy who was experiencing his very first plane flight. He was in the window seat, peering out the porthole, narrating everything to his mom, who was sitting between us. He enthusiastically described the size and shape of every piece of luggage that was crawling up the conveyor belt into the belly of our aircraft. Then he squealed with excitement when another jet pulled up into the gate next to ours, and began to describe that plane's particulars. His voice increased in volume during our taxi and take-off to an almost screeching level, and I found myself sighing and thinking, *This is going to be a* really *long flight.* However, once we were in the air, he was curiously silent.

I glanced over his mother's magazine to make sure he hadn't swallowed a peanut or something and was graced by the sight of a six-year-old in awe. His eyes were wide and his mouth formed a silent "Oh!" Seeing his cherubic face illuminated with wonder, I realized that I'd evolved into a very jaded frequent flyer. Riding in winged metal tubes is something I do to get from one city to another. I hardly even notice the scenery anymore. What that little boy considered to be a miracle has become a mundane reality to me. My awe has been usurped by *apathy*.

One of Jesus' harshest rebukes was aimed at *spiritual* apathy:

> I know your deeds, that you are neither cold nor hot. I wish you were either one or the other! So, because you are lukewarm—neither hot nor cold—I am about to spit you out of my mouth (Revelation 3:15-16).

Those severe words were directed at a first-century church plant in a place called Laodicea. Archaeologists tell us this city was known for its banks, textile industry and the manufacture of a unique eye ointment, which was a big seller in drugstores throughout Asia Minor.

Squinting tourists flocked to Laodicea to pay homage to the lime-rich spring water, which was the active ingredient in this early version of Visine. They paid a dollar for a map and a trolley ride to the river, then hopped off expecting to see a beautiful, flowing stream. What they found instead was a tepid, slow moving trickle, choked with green slime.

But the people living there didn't care that their water source was gross, because they got rich off it. The "miracle drops" paid for their fancy homes and foreign cars and giant plasma screen TVs. But their preoccupation with materialism led to a loss of spiritual passion: *I mean really, who cares about going to hear some guy talk about taking up your cross daily or washing other people's nasty feet when you can stay home in your pajamas and watch a movie on a big screen with surround sound?* Or so they thought.

I wonder if they were jolted from their spiritual stupor when they got John's dog-eared letter—with the none-too-subtle "lukewarm" reference—accusing them of rolling their eyes at God. I wonder what kind of buzz went through their well-dressed crowd when they heard that their laxity made Jesus gag. More important, I wonder if they accepted His undeserved offer of forgiveness and restoration:

> Those whom I love I rebuke and discipline. So be earnest, and repent. Here I am! I stand at the door and knock. If anyone hears my voice and opens the door, I will come in and eat with him, and he with me (Revelation 3:19-20).

I think those verses are a fitting end to this supernatural love story God narrated for us. They paint a beautiful portrait of our sharing a meal with our Savior. They describe an intimate rapport between us and our Redeemer. In spite of our rebellion, fickle faith and self-centeredness, *the Creator of the Universe wants to be close to us.* And that relationship with Jesus is the only thing that will truly satisfy the cry of our heart. He is our peace. He is our living hope.

What's the *Story* of This Particular Book?

Despite best-selling novels and differing doctrines about the end of times, the "apocalypse" isn't the central theme of Revelation. *Redemption is.* In a nutshell, this series of prophetic visions John recorded while exiled on the rocky Greek island of Patmos points to the ultimate victory we Christians will experience as we stand with our Savior, Jesus. There will be a final colossal battle (which began in Eden) between good and evil, and our Redeemer will reign supreme. Satan gets his butt kicked once and for all. Then we get to spend eternity with the God who created us, restored us and loves us!

Henrietta's Highlights on Revelation

Her Synopsis
Revelation Portrays Jesus Christ, Our Triumphant King

Her Suggested Bible Readings

Sunday:	*Christ and the Churches* (Revelation 1–3)
Monday:	*Christ's Throne and the Seven Sealed Book* (Revelation 4–6)
Tuesday:	*Christ's Trumpets Sounded* (Revelation 7–9)
Wednesday:	*Christ and the Woes* (Revelation 10–12)
Thursday:	*Christ and the Antichrist* (Revelation 13–15)
Friday:	*Christ's Final Triumph* (Revelation 16–18)
Saturday:	*Christ the Lord of All* (Revelation 19–22)

Memorable Quotes from Dr. Mears
"Revelation is the only book of prophecy in the New Testament. It is the only book in the divine library that especially promises a blessing to those who read and hear."

"Revelation presents a glorious, reigning Christ. The Gospels present Him as a Savior, One who came to take the curse of sin, but in this last book we see no humiliation."

"Yes, God's story ends, 'and they lived happily ever after.'"

Looking for Yourself in God's Love Story

1. Read Revelation 1:13-16. Using John's description as a template, what adjectives would you use to describe a glorified, triumphant Jesus?

2. Read Revelation 4. I've also heard "heaven" concisely described as "a place where there will be no more crying and no more dying." What are you most curious about when you contemplate what heaven will be like?

3. The hopeful themes resonating throughout the book of Revelation are that Jesus wins the final battle between good and evil, and that we get to be united with Him forever. What's the first thing you'd like to say when you finally get to see your loving Savior face to face?

Movie Clip Moment

I couldn't begin to find a movie clip adequate for the supernatural hope that echoes throughout this last book of the Bible, but I did find a wonderful film with a running theme of redemption. The storyline includes sorrow because someone dies and joy because someone's saved—which, come to think of it, is not unlike John's vision of unrepentant sinners being separated from God for all eternity, while those of us who believe will experience everlasting life. Our final flick is titled *Life Is Beautiful* (1997), a more than appropriate sentiment as we come to the end of God's living letter to us.

Endnotes

1. Paul Taylor Udouj, "A Country Boy Can Survive," © Paul Udouj, First by Ten Publishing, Fort Smith, Arkansas.
2. Brennan Manning, from remarks at First Presbyterian Church, Winston-Salem, NC, Nov. 18-20, 1990, as told in Alan Wright, *Lover of My Soul* (Sisters, OR: Multnomah Publishers, 1998), pp. 104-105.
3. Dietrich Bonhoeffer, *The Cost of Discipleship* (New York: Macmillan Press, 1959).
4. A. W. Tozer, *The Pursuit of God* (Colorado Springs, CO: Christian Publications, Inc: 1948).
5. Hoyt Axton, "Joy to the World (Jeremiah Was a Bullfrog)."
6. Eric Olson, Paul Verna and Carlo Wolff, eds., *The Encyclopedia of Record Producers: An Indispensable Guide to the Most Important Record Producers in Music History* (New York: Billboard Books, 1999).

For speaking/booking inquires please contact:

Ambassador Speakers Bureau
(615) 370-4700
Info@AmbassadorSpeakers.com
www.AmbassadorSpeakers.com

You can also contact Lisa directly at:
www.lisaharper.net